Get Running

Mary Jennings

GILL BOOKS

Gill Books
Hume Avenue
Park West
Dublin 12
www.gillbooks.ie

Gill Books is an imprint of M.H. Gill and Co.

978 07171 8376 0

Designed by Jane Matthews
Edited by Susan McKeever
Proofread by Jane Rogers
Printed by GraphyCems, Spain

Photos on pp. 3 and 247 courtesy of Donal Glackin/*Irish Runner Magazine*;
p. 25 courtesy of Gráinne Mac Giolla Rí; p. 107 (top right) courtesy of
Veronica Rahneberg; pp. 118 and 179 courtesy of *The Irish Times*; pp. 115 and
201 courtesy of Beaujolais International Marathon; pp. 123 and 193 courtesy
of Tom Coppinger; p. 129 courtesy of Jetline Action Photo; p. 145 courtesy
of Aideen Kelly; p. 187 courtesy of Eoin Fegan; pp. 188–89 courtesy of Sean
Griffin; pp. 219 and 239 courtesy of FinisherPix L.L.C.; p. 231 courtesy of
Maindru Photo.

5 4 3 2 1

About the Author

Having discovered running in her early twenties, Mary was amazed at the difference it made to her life. Not coming from a sporty background, it was a revelation to be able to enjoy running as an adult. After eight years of enjoying the freedom of running while working as a management consultant, Mary made the decision to leave her corporate job and follow her passion. She retrained as a personal trainer and decided to focus her attention on supporting others to take up running without being intimidated by it.

Mary founded ForgetTheGym.ie in 2007 to encourage new runners to get outside, try running and feel great. Today Mary coaches runners of all levels. She writes a regular column in the *Irish Times* and has appeared on Irish radio and television. As a keen long-distance runner, Mary has completed over 45 marathons and ultra-marathons up to 100km in distance. Mary believes that exercise should be fun, enjoyable and pain-free.

She is a Chi Running technique instructor and holds an MSc in Exercise and Sports Psychology from the University of Ulster. Before the running bug took hold, Mary studied at Dublin City University and ESC Reims in France. She attained a double degree of BA in European Business and Diplôme d'Etudes Supérieures Européennes de Management (DESEM). Today she mainly uses her French to organise running holidays in the region. Mary lives in Dublin with her husband, John, and young son, Harry.

Acknowledgements

There would be no book if it were not for those who shared their passion for running with me over the past 18 years. Thank you to all who have encouraged me to get running and to continue to search out new ways of making running more enjoyable, fun and full of adventure.

I feel so honoured that I can continue to pass on my love of running to others. To everyone who has volunteered their stories, photos and inspiration for this book, I thank you. To the runners, coaches and enthusiastic supporters at ForgetTheGym.ie, this book is for you. You are the people who I have learned most from and who continue to be inspired by each day. It is a pleasure to have such a wonderful 'running family'.

Thank you to everyone who encouraged me to write and supported me with advice and tips. I am especially grateful to the *Irish Times*, who took a chance on me in 2014 by asking me to design their online running programmes. To this day they allow me to share my running ramblings in their paper. I would never have considered writing about running without the confidence that the wonderful team of editors have had in my ability to do so over the past five years.

Combining running, coaching and writing has become my new career, but it does take a lot of time and dedication, no matter how much it doesn't feel like a 'real' job. I'd be lost without the behind-the-scenes support of my husband, parents, family and friends for embracing the 'running madness' by cheerleading at events, listening to all the ups and downs, but most especially for working overtime by babysitting little Harry over this last year while I put pen to paper to write this book.

I hope the book encourages you all to enjoy running, accept the times when it will take a back seat in your life, and embrace it when it can take centre stage.

Here's to many more miles to come.
Mary

Note

This book is written as a source of information only and is not intended to be taken as a replacement for medical advice. A qualified medical practitioner should always be consulted before beginning any new diet, exercise or health plan.

Introduction

I love running and I am so lucky that it is not only my hobby and my passion but also my job. This wasn't always the way. During school and early adulthood, I did little to no exercise and thought that runners were a strange breed. After years of avoiding PE classes, I had accepted that the world was divided into sporty people and non-sporty people and I was quite comfortable being in the latter camp.

However, once I was (reluctantly) introduced to running in my mid-twenties, I couldn't believe how it impacted my wellbeing, confidence and energy. I well and truly got the bug and in 2006 ended up leaving a perfectly good but stressful job as a management consultant, and retraining as a personal trainer and running coach.

I understand how hard it is for people who have so many commitments in life to try to fit in running. We are all time-poor and our own health and wellbeing often get shifted down the to-do list even when we do have the very best of intentions. We tend to prioritise family, work, housework and maybe even Netflix ahead of our own bodies.

I started Forget The Gym in 2007 to make it easier for people to start running, enjoy the fresh air, take a little time for themselves and feel amazing. I began by coaching friends and family who had seen and heard how running had changed my life. Over the past twelve years Forget The Gym has grown thanks to a wonderful community of students and running coaches.

At Forget The Gym we aim to replace the competition in running with camaraderie. None of us is going to qualify for the Olympics so the only person we really need to compete with is our own self. There's no focus on weight loss or measuring tapes; instead I aim to make people feel better by encouraging them to improve from where they are now and get them out running comfortably and effortlessly.

One of the best perks of the job is that I get to run and be outside while I work. I'm not a natural athlete who jumps out of bed in the morning and wants to go running before breakfast. Like many other recreational runners, while I love the feeling after a run, it can take me a long time to build up to getting out the door. I procrastinate until the last minute or maybe even until another day. Being the teacher thankfully means I can't make excuses. I just have to get up and go. I never regret it either.

I want to show you how to get rid of your excuses, make running something you want to do and begin a healthy lifelong habit that you love. Running is better than any diet, and once you catch the running bug I promise you will wonder how you ever lived without it. If I can do it, you certainly can too.

1

WHY RUNNING?

If you are not a runner (yet), you may wonder what the attraction is. From the outside running must seem like a very boring hobby indeed. Constantly putting one foot in front of another for minutes and possibly even hours? How is that in any way exciting? But talk to any runner and you'll realise that running offers a lot more to an individual than just a means of getting from A to B.

We all run for different reasons:
- Some runners train to win races and push their bodies as far as they can.
- Some people run for health and weight-loss reasons.
- Many runners use running as a way to escape – to reduce stress and clear their heads of their worries and responsibilities.

Whatever their reason to run, most runners are passionate about how running makes them feel and are keen to encourage others to give it a try.

Running is my way of feeling free and enjoying the fresh air. I return home positive, enthusiastic and energised. I feel strong and capable and clearer in my head. I feel like my day is a success even if I have done nothing else but run. I may not be the fastest runner, but speed is not the priority in my running. I love how running makes me feel afterwards and also the friendships and opportunities for travel and adventure it has offered me.

I never envisaged how much I would enjoy the social side of running. Whether it is the company of a friend on a leisurely weekend run, the exchange of a smile and a nod with a passing runner in the park, the buzz of taking part in a marathon or the simple joy of coaching a group of runners to their first 5k, the camaraderie of fellow runners is priceless.

Growing up, the only runners I was aware of were 'athletes'. They were members of an athletic club, comfortable in short shorts and very competitive. Running was about winning races, getting faster and pushing themselves to their limits. I don't remember knowing anyone who ran purely as a leisure pursuit. But in recent years there has been a significant growth in the number of people running for fun.

While certain runners continue to run for peak performance and podium places, more of us are happy to run just for ourselves and take on challenges with a little less dedication than those at the top. This more relaxed bunch are what we call 'recreational runners' and there are a lot of us out there. Many have taken up running in their adult years and their focus is very different from that of the competitive athlete.

We all know someone who is the 'unlikely runner'; someone who was never sporty and is now taking part in races and events and is passionate about how running makes them feel. Running has a strange power of taking hold of our perceptions of our capabilities and makes us realise that we are able to do a lot more than we think. The increased self-belief, pride and resilience leads to a more positive mindset overall.

While many recreational runners start out running for health, fitness or weight-loss reasons, most runners keep it up for another reason. It's only when you start running regularly that you realise the main added bonus of running. Running has a powerful way of offering headspace. Running can reduce a temper or lift a bad mood. There are also benefits from running that have nothing to do with our physical or mental wellbeing. Something as simple as the discipline of following a training schedule and structuring a season of training has taught many of us how to set goals, follow a plan and deal with setbacks along the way. This can then be applied to many other areas of our lives.

> 'I started running when my dad died and it definitely helped me through a very tough time. I enjoyed the physical benefits, but the value of the psychological benefits are immeasurable. Running really helped to get me out of the house, clear my head and take care of myself. And most of all, I actually had some fun!' **Liz**

Reasons to Run

We all have our own reasons for running and they are what drive us to keep it going and want to continue running for many years to come.

Feilim's story

At eighteen, Feilim started running with his mum Ailbhe and dad Eoin. Ailbhe admits she never thought she would run. Being over fifty, she had assumed she was too old to start. Feilim has autism and she was keen to get him involved in some form of exercise. He wanted to be with her, so she had to put on her running shoes and go with him to ensure he ran too. Following the plan, all three of the family made it to their first 5k, crossing the finish line together, one of Ailbhe's greatest running memories. That event kick-started something special as now Ailbhe admits she might just have become a little bit addicted to running. Running has brought some welcome bonuses for the family. Ailbhe explains how running has made such a difference to Feilim's whole demeanour and mood, calming him at times of stress. He is also a lot fitter. As a family, the peer pressure works great too for motivation because if one of them goes running they all go, so it's hard to make excuses. As a mum, the real reward for Ailbhe is at the finish line of the races, seeing the huge smile and sense of achievement on Feilim's face when he finishes a race and gets his medal. Within a few years Ailbhe and her family have used running to help them build their relationships, fitness and wellbeing all by just putting on their running shoes.

'I am a much nicer person once I've had my run.'
Caroline

'Running offers me-time and a chance to do something truly for myself.'
Jane

'Running has brought me the most amazing friends and it has even got me a husband!'
Hayley

'Running helps me clear my head, spend time with friends and gives me a wonderful sense of peace and accomplishment.'
Deirdre

'Running gives a sense of achievement, confidence and an amazing atmosphere/buzz at events (especially for those of us down the back!).'
Aileen

'Running creates a natural high and things that seemed complicated or annoying before getting out seem a lot less so after the run.'
Sarah

'Running gives me time and space to generate ideas, make decisions, chat to running buddies or do it all.'
Emma

'Forget The Gym'

Let's be clear. I am not anti-gym. If you enjoy the gym and you are motivated to go then please keep going. There are great exercises, classes and trainers that come with a gym membership. That is, if you actually turn up. It's very easy to buy a gym membership but it's a lot harder to be a consistent gym-goer. Gyms can be intimidating places full of beautiful bodies and complicated machines and if you are self-conscious or lacking in confidence as well as fitness, often the gym can become the place that you feel guilty avoiding rather than somewhere you look forward to attending.

I have exercised outdoors for so long now that exercising indoors feels claustrophobic. I love the fresh air and the clarity and freedom that being outdoors brings. If you too are a little gym shy, remember there is a whole gym on your doorstep if you look outside the window. The hardest bit, like any exercise regime, is getting started. Once you walk or run outside, a treadmill is never quite the same again. From park benches to trails, steps to lamp posts, you can create your own 'green gym' workout. The fresh air clears the head and lifts the spirits – I find that my best ideas come to me when I'm out for a run. It's not just me who finds this either – studies in Britain, Scandinavia and the United States are consistently finding that people exercising outdoors display higher vitality, energy, enthusiasm and self-esteem than when they perform the equivalent exercise indoors. In virtually all of the studies, they also show signs of lower fatigue, tension and depression after an outdoor activity.

I miss it when I don't get outside; sunny days stuck in an office drove me to leave my desk-bound job and set up Forget The Gym. I dreamt of a job where I could be in the driving seat and choose to be outdoors when I wanted. It was not a particular love for exercise, but more a love for the freedom of the great outdoors. Getting outside at whatever pace is right for you today is the best thing you can do to enhance your life.

Less Stress, More Fun

I remember asking one of my running students how she was feeling about running. She told me that it was her running anniversary and guess what she said? 'I'm two years older but ten years younger.'

Running needs to be fun, yet many people take it too seriously. Put simply, if we don't enjoy it, we won't keep it up. If running becomes a chore, it joins the long list of things we feel we should be doing but never get time to do properly. Instead we need to start seeing it as a privilege and an honour to be able to get out the door.

Running doesn't have to always be about keeping up with others. We have enough stress in our days without running adding to it. Yet I see a lot of runners anxious and disillusioned with running because they have perceptions of where they should be as a runner and constantly compare themselves with other runners. They overtrain and burn out. What is the point in running if it is going to bring such anxiety with it?

While there are times when pushing our bodies to reach a personal best time or a longer distance is right for us, the number of kilometres, or the time on the clock should not always be the most important thing. It's true that we thrive on that feeling of progress when we get faster and stronger, but there is a fine line between pushing ourselves and getting injured. For running to be a lifelong fun activity we need to look after our bodies, treat them with respect, reward them for the hard work put in, and sometimes give them a kick in the right direction when feeling a little lazy.

My Coaching Philosophy

I know it's hard to make the time for running – I'll admit I've also used most of the excuses my students give me not to run. Running would rarely reach the top of my to-do list if I didn't enlist some helpful tips and tricks to get me to drop what I'm doing and go running. We all need a gentle push out the door to go running sometimes and that's what I aim to provide to all my running students, including you.

When I started coaching runners back in 2006, my goal was to help people start running and build towards 5k. However, twelve years on I realise that coaching running involves a lot more than helping people become better runners. By getting people running, meeting other runners and supporting each other to reach new goals, my role now is to help people feel better about themselves. Most of the feedback I have received relates to how the running achievements have actually made people more confident and realise how capable they are in many areas of their lives, not just running. Doing something we never thought possible can change our mindset on who we think we are, what we think we can do and what opportunities are available to us. Running is merely the tool that helps the individual shine.

As a coach, I identify the starting point for each runner, create a realistic plan with their lifestyle in mind and support them through the ups and downs. My favourite part of coaching is of course being there to celebrate with them when they do reach the impossible. Whether a runner is a complete beginner or training for a marathon I believe that if you prepare them well, build their confidence as well as their fitness and strength they are more likely to enjoy running, keep on running and challenge themselves to try new adventures that might currently be outside their comfort zone.

Whether your impossible is a thirty-minute run or a marathon, you have to start from where you are right now, being realistic yet positive about where you need to go. Often the end goal is impossible to

imagine, so I tend to get my runners to concentrate just on the week they are in and identify what they can do this week to help bring them closer to their goal. They will have the big picture in the back of their head, but it can be too intimidating to focus on that all the time. Looking at what we are able to do this week makes our goal more manageable, possible and a little less scary.

When we see others succeed and achieve similar goals it can make us realise that 'if they can do it, then surely I can too'. Having support is paramount as negative voices speak a lot louder than positive ones for a runner. We will all hit setbacks; it's how we choose to handle these setbacks that counts. Applying basic sports psychology, project management and some general common sense to our running is the difference between just running kilometres and really making a difference to what we achieve.

I want to help you to tap into your running potential and maybe a whole new unknown that is out there waiting for you.

Who Is This Book For?

Whether you are a beginner who wants to get started or a lapsed runner who wants to reignite their love for running, this book will offer you some practical advice and inspiration to help you make running an enjoyable and positive part of your life.

If you enjoy competition there is plenty of opportunity to challenge yourself, but running doesn't always have to be a race to see who is the fastest or strongest. There are no rules: we make our own rules. Stop for coffee along the way, find a new route, run alone, run with a group, do whatever makes you smile. Running can be whatever you want it to be.

In this book I'm going to coach you in the way I would coach one of my running students:

- I will ask you a set of questions to find out where you are at and where you are going.
- I will give you tips, inspiration and hopefully a laugh or two as you progress.
- I will be a virtual support to you every step of the way.

By the end of the book I will end up in your head when you go running. I'll be with you, the positive voice that replaces any negative thoughts that are holding you back.

No matter what level of runner you are, there is always something new to learn. Most of the lessons of running I have learnt have come from other runners and mistakes I have made myself.

1 For the New Runner

I want to introduce you to running, guide you sensibly and gradually from walking all the way to running 5k while making sure you enjoy it, appreciate it and maybe surprise yourself with what you can achieve.

2 For the Lapsed Runner

I want to reignite your love for running and remind you of the reasons you enjoyed it. I aim to help you find your running mojo and this time make running a regular habit and an enjoyable part of your life that you will never want to give up again.

3 For the Regular Runner

I want to make sure you can continue to reap the benefits of running for many more years to come. I will show you how you can add new components to your training, avoid injury and maintain your running passion and enthusiasm by looking at running a little differently.

2

THE SUCCESSFUL RUNNER

What Is Success?

If I asked you to name a 'successful' runner you would most likely think of an elite athlete, an Olympian or someone who has achieved great feats. Yet while success can indeed mean medals and records, most of us recreational runners find it hard to relate to elite athlete drive and determination. Thankfully, there is no rule to say that in order to be successful we need to be aiming for the top. A successful runner doesn't always have to be the one who is the fastest and strongest. Some of the most inspiring runners I know are those who have overcome illness or grief or have persevered through many setbacks to build up to 5k without stopping. So what are the characteristics that make up a successful runner?

- A successful runner is someone who is consistent, motivated and adaptable.
- A successful runner has one eye on future running plans but at the same time is grateful for their ability to run today.
- A successful runner is most likely following a training plan and has a notebook full of running memories and old training plans.
- A successful runner is someone who inspires and supports other runners with their enthusiasm and understanding.
- A successful runner looks after their body, their mind and their running buddies.
- A successful runner knows when to push their body and when to take a break.

This is the type of runner I aspire to be.

How we define a 'great' or 'successful' runner is a very individual thing. Realistically, unless running is your job and you are in it for the medals, how you define being a 'good runner' really is no one else's business other than your own.

What type of runner do you want to be, and do you know any runner you aspire to be like?

The Grand Plan

In our careers we often spend a lot of time planning our schedules, goals and professional futures. Have you ever considered planning like this for your running 'career'?

Without making plans a year can disappear and we have no idea where it has gone. Without planning for our 'running future' we risk letting time, life and everyone else's priorities take over something that is incredibly valuable to our wellbeing.

With a work background in project management I love the exercise of sitting down to plan. Each year I take some time out plan my running year on paper. I book in races, sign up to courses and plan holidays around those dates. At the end of each running year I look back on the highlights and what worked and what didn't. I think sometimes I enjoy the planning and the anticipation of running events as much as the training itself! A year can fly by quickly, but it's much easier to achieve more in a year if it is on paper. It's also very therapeutic to look back, look forward and use both of those views to tailor what we do today.

Take a Look Back

Before we start planning for the future, take a moment to remember all you have achieved so far in running. If you have never run before, you have a clean slate. However, many of you are reading this reminiscing about good runs in the past, sprints to finish lines and post-run celebrations. Think about what you enjoy about running and how running makes you feel. What are your biggest accomplishments to date and what lessons have you learnt from running?

Most recreational runners never plan on retiring. They want to be able to enjoy it, stay motivated and still take on new challenges for many years to come. Whatever your distance, pace or focus right now, wouldn't it be great to know that running might always be there for you to guide you through life?

The Vision

Where do you see yourself in ten years' time?

Ironically it was this very question that made me look at the career path I was on, change things radically and end up sitting at my kitchen table writing this book. At a career path workshop in my management consultancy job we were asked to map out our future from our current position to the desirable top position of partner. As I sat there doodling on the paper I realised that being partner really didn't interest me at all. Even though my forties were fifteen years away at that stage, the dream of the big salary and the powerful job didn't really appeal. I couldn't understand how I would get to have any free time or flexibility in my work schedule if that was to be my path.

I was in the type of job where there was a lot of travel and uncertainty about work locations. While it was exciting at first, the novelty of hotel breakfasts and early morning flights wore off quickly and I realised how impossible it was to commit to any extracurricular nurturing activities. Honestly, if I had not sat down to do that planning exercise I'm pretty certain that I would have stayed on that original career path. I had great friends and the longer I remained in that circle, the more normal it would have become and the harder it would have been to jump ship.

I secured a one-year career break which meant I didn't have to take any big leaps. Yes, I feel very lucky to have my own path now, but I am also lucky to have had the career I had before as the lessons learnt there are what helped me build a business, a loyal customer base and a career that fits in with my grand plan. I have a huge amount to thank PwC and IBM for all I learnt there – the project management skills I acquired there helped hugely in setting up my business. Added to that were the computer skills I used to create a website, the admin skills I used keep the business going and the presentation skills I used to deliver talks to groups. I also developed the kind of confidence that only comes from being thrown in at the deep end to challenging jobs where the only option was sink or swim. Most important, I had first-hand experience of how years at a desk job can impact our body and our motivation. I know how hard it is to make time for fitness and health when work is stressful. I've been there too.

Wherever you are right now, you have lessons learnt and experience you can bring to your future. You might not be able to drop your job completely, but there are opportunities everywhere, whether it is to help out initially with volunteering or surrounding yourself with people who do the things they love. I for one would never ever have assumed I would have been running and writing as a career. How ironic (and gratifying) fifteen years later to be back delivering corporate talks on wellbeing and the stress-releasing benefits of running to the same employer that kickstarted my career.

Dream Big?

It's hard to stay on the right track if you have no clue where you are heading. Have you got any big running goals? Or maybe even some small ones? Having a goal is a key step in getting some structure into your running routine. A goal, a plan and the anticipation of a great achievement to come is what keeps many people motivated and running long into the future. Goals could include:

- Getting faster
- Running for longer
- The ability to keep on running injury-free long term
- Completing a particular event
- Achieving a personal best time
- Being able to run after your kids.

With a concrete goal to aim for, it will be easier to get out on the days when you cannot really find the reason or motivation to run. We all have the opportunity to achieve more with a bit of planning and dedication.

Choose Your Running Goals

Do you see yourself as a runner in the future? If so, let's make it real. Try to visualise yourself running this time next month, next year and in a few years' time. Consider even ten years from now. What type of running will you be doing and what races or goals will you have? Will you be running alone or with others? If you can picture it then you can start to work towards it. This exercise is strangely addictive so don't blame me if you end up booking races and coming up with exciting new challenges today.

Be inspired by some of the running goals that my students have for the future:

Avoid injury

Be more confident

Eat better for running

Become a morning runner

Run a half marathon

Find a running buddy

Run on holiday Run with my dog

Improve my technique

Join a running group

Run abroad

Set a personal best (PB) time or distance target

Be a parkrun regular

Do fifty parkruns Run abroad

Get faster

Run for charity Stay consistent

Be more confident

Run three times per week

Breathe better when running

Join an online community

Volunteer

Run with kids

Enjoy running

Run on mountains

Go off-road

Run 10km

Get stronger

Do fifty parkruns

Prioritise myself

Stretch

Win a race

Run 5km non-stop

Run a marathon

Strength train

Become a coach Run on a track

Running Goals

Here are a few examples that might help you choose realistic yet exciting challenges for you.

This Year	Next Year	Long Term – Some Day
Jack To start back running/ walking regularly three times per week. To do one parkrun a month. To stop worrying about the time on the clock, and just get out the door for now.	To run parkrun any week I'm free, non-stop, and aim to get faster, stronger and more consistent over the distance. To find a 10k and follow a plan to get there from 5k.	To keep running regularly, to do a few 10ks per year and one parkrun per month to keep me moving and motivated. To keep volunteering at parkruns when I can.
Fiona To recover from injury, building back to 10k in the next three months. To look into joining a running club for support and motivation.	To be a member of a running club or at least have a few running buddies who I run with weekly. To enjoy running 10ks and hopefully get faster over this distance.	To build up to a half marathon and maybe even a marathon … who knows! But I know I need to look after my body now if this will be on the cards. I don't want to be injured again.
Paula To complete my first marathon this year. To run four times per week and keep up my one swimming and one gym session which I find helps me feel better when running.	Based on how I feel after the marathon, maybe consider another one, but will give myself some time to reflect on the marathon and see how that changes my opinion on running.	To be still enjoying running, still be in contact with my running buddies and still be comfortable over long and short distances doing events in new places with groups and on my own.

My Running Goals
Now it is over to you to put your dreams on paper ...

This Year	Next Year	Long Term – Some Day

The Next Eight Weeks

Regardless of whatever grand plans you have for your running over the next few years, you won't reach these long-term goals if you don't start with the first very basic steps. Consider what you could achieve over the next eight weeks that would get you on the right track for your long-term goal. Eight weeks is long enough for most people to plan but short enough to keep us passionate, focused and motivated.

You can change a lot in eight weeks.
- As a beginner you can move from walker to 5k runner.
- As a 5k runner you can move to being a 10k runner.
- As a lapsed runner you can get back into the routine and get your 5k comfortable and enjoyable again.
- As a runner who would like to move towards long distance, you can get the groundwork well in place.

There will always be other things in life that will fill your spare time if you let them. However, so many of these distractions won't matter in the long term and you will wonder where the time went.

Don't let another month of this year sneak by unnoticed. Pick the running goals that appeal to you from the word cloud on page 29 and think about what is possible with the life and commitments you have right now. We can never be sure of what the future can bring but we can try to picture our ideal running future. Be detailed in your short-term goals and a little more open-minded in the long-term ones.

> Your goal needs to remain in a prominent place – stuck to the fridge, on your desktop or by the front door, for instance. It helps to be reminded all the time where you are going and why it is important to you. Otherwise it will shift further down your to-do list until it becomes something that you feel guilty for never getting the time to do.

Filling the Gaps

Once you have your goals on paper, the next step is to break them down into what you can do right now. Think about your next eight weeks and what time you have available. Ideally three to four training sessions per week will be

Here is your clean slate.

	MONDAY	TUESDAY	WEDNESDAY
1			
2			
3			
4			
5			
6			
7			
8			

plenty. If you think that is not enough, fear not; there are plenty more things I will suggest you do to complement your running. Throughout the next chapters there are training plans, guidelines and tips for how you can create your own training plan. We all have different starting points and aspirations. But we all need to start somewhere.

THURSDAY	FRIDAY	SATURDAY	SUNDAY

Beginners

If you have never run you can head straight to Chapter 3 which will guide you on your path.

Chapter 3

Lapsed Runners

It might be so long since you have put your running shoes on that you don't even know how long you can run for today. That's okay. Go out for a walk/run and see how many minutes you can run for slowly before wanting to stop. You will then have defined your starting point. Chapter 4 will guide you on how to progress from there.

Chapter 4

Already Running

If you are running regularly you know where your starting point is. You know what fits in with your lifestyle and what motivates you to keep going. All you need now is to find your goal and be able to work out your plan to reach it. From Chapter 6 onwards you will find tips and inspiration to help you get more out of your running.

Chapter 6 7 8

3

START OUT
RIGHT

Deirdre's running story

So, sitting on my couch one night, I saw an offer for a 'learn to run' class. Weighing in at nearly sixteen stone, the most exercise I got was typing, I was reluctant but knew something had to change.

I turned up in July 2011 for an eight-week Couch to 5k course. I didn't even own a track suit. There is no doubt that the class was tough. The first day, a light jog of one minute left me absolutely breathless. I was sore the next day and even more sore the following day. But there was such a good atmosphere in the class. The first time we completed the thirty-minute run, Mary turned to us and said, 'You see, you can do anything if you put your mind to it'. It was, beyond a doubt, the most powerful and scary thing I have ever heard. I realised that whatever I wanted to do was absolutely achievable if I put my mind to it.

I slowly started realising that running was changing my life in every way. I became more organised in work, I was thinking better, clearer almost and physically I had, albeit with the help of a very strict diet, dropped five stone. People didn't recognise me. I didn't recognise me! And the only exercise I was doing was the plan with Forget The Gym.

Running has changed my life quite literally. I got promoted in work, and I put this partly down to running. Following that, I got an opportunity to take up a job in Paris for four years. And now, running is keeping me sane while I'm settling in, here in a country where I don't speak the language! I'm sure I look like an Irish nutter in my Forget The Gym T-shirt, doing my own version of our classes around the Eiffel Tower once a week!

But running has made me realise that it doesn't matter what anyone else thinks, who cares if some else is faster, slower, thinner, better.

Running has taught me about motivation, endurance and reward. If it's not hard, you won't get a buzz after it. But that buzz is worth it. So if you are even considering it, if there's even a glimmer of a maybe, do it.

'I Can't Run'

I've heard it all before; I spent many years telling myself the exact same thing. It is amazing how we create a story in our heads that is most likely based on our experience of sport in school or a few attempts of breathless sprinting around the park.

If you have tried running before but have failed to progress with it, consider once again why you might not have succeeded.

- Was it how you approached running? Maybe you started out too fast, skipped a warm up or didn't wear the right gear.
- Could you have possibly done too much too soon?
- Did you set yourself a target that was too far advanced for your fitness level?
- Did you compare yourself with others rather than your own past running experience?

If you have fooled yourself into thinking you are not a runner I encourage you to look at running in a new light and attempt running with a different mindset. Only if you are still not convinced after that will I allow you retire your running shoes.

> 'I have just finished Mary's beginners' running programme and ran my thirty minutes twice this week to believe it was real. It's such a big personal accomplishment for me that it reminds me of passing my driving test. Mary and her team have motivated me every step of the way with no scary stuff or punishing regimes – just purely made me feel I had it in me.' **Nickie**

If you have any underlying medical conditions or feel that your health or your age might not be what it used to be, make sure you have your doctor's approval to start building up. Bring along the training plan below and show them what you are attempting. They will see how gradual the programme is and hopefully will wish you the best with it. Certainly, if you feel any pain when running, please stop immediately.

Why Do You Want to Become a Runner?

Maybe you have smug running friends who do nothing but talk about how amazing running makes them feel. You might be starting to run as a personal challenge or have long wished to start running but never found the right time. Health or weight-loss reasons might be your driver for getting running. Whatever is inspiring you to run right now, take a moment to make a note of it. You can store it in your phone, on a fancy spreadsheet or even in the margin of this book, but make sure it's somewhere you will see it often. Very quickly you will forget what life was like before running and it's lovely to have this little reminder of the 'old' you and why starting running was important to you.

Why do I want to run?

Doing It Right

Running often gets a bad name because many people launch into ambitious training plans without paying any attention to their bodies and get injured by doing too much too soon. Having coached runners of all levels for over twelve years, I continually meet new runners who have become frustrated about their attempts to run. They generally all have a similar experience and have made the key mistakes that many new runners make.

I'm going to show you how to avoid their mistakes and help you build a solid foundation that will set you on the best path to becoming the runner you want to be.

> *'Running is now integral to my life and apart from keeping fit, sane and in shape, I have met some great people as a result of it. Thanks Mary for inspiring me to join the world of recreational runners!'* **Suzanne**

A Sensible Way to Start

- **BUILD UP GRADUALLY:** Running to exhaustion doesn't help the runner mentally or physically at this early stage. Accept that your body will take a little time to adapt to becoming a runner so alternate walking and running throughout your first weeks of training. Over time you will be surprised at how quickly the body will adjust, but give it an opportunity to build strength, fitness and stamina at its own pace.

- **KEEP IT SIMPLE:** If exercise is too complicated or time-consuming, it is easy to make excuses and give up. The key is to start small and build up a routine of manageable runs at a pace right for you. Each week you will be motivated by your progress and that will encourage you to keep going. Aim for no more than three training sessions per week to give your body time to recover from each session and prepare for the next. Follow my training plan for beginners rather than run aimlessly (see page 50).

- **SLOW DOWN:** Many new runners feel like they should be running at a pace where they are breathless. Learning to run is not about sprinting or pushing your body to its limits. This leads to tension and general discomfort. When starting out run at a pace where you can comfortably breathe and talk at the same time. It may not be fast, but that is not what is important right now. The pace will increase as our fitness and strength does. A minute is still a minute; it won't go any faster if you run faster. Save the fast runs for the future when your body has become accustomed to running.

- **BELIEVE:** Many new runners don't feel like 'real' runners and tend to look down and bend a little at the waist. They often lack confidence and can feel embarrassed running in public. Physically this reduces their lung capability, which makes breathing hard and also requires the legs to work more. Add to this the mental weight of self-doubt and it's no wonder many people question their ability to become a runner. Even if you are not confident, fake it. Stand tall and look straight ahead when you run. Your body will carry itself better, you will have more lung space for air and you will feel lighter on your feet.

- **GET SUPPORT:** If you know you will struggle to stay motivated alone, look around for someone else who may have the same goal. Ask them to meet you for a run, or maybe even a walk to start. It only takes two of you to start a group. All you need is some enthusiasm and a joint commitment to keep each other on track. After that, the magic happens and who knows where it might take you? If you can't find someone to go with you, then find a friend or family member who will 'encourage' you to get out the door, especially on the days when you will be thinking up excuses to skip a run. We tend to be more likely to commit if we have promised someone else we will go.

- **DON'T COMPETE:** Do not compare your fitness, progress or speed with other runners. Every person starting out running is different, so don't waste your energy focusing on how you compare with them. Instead think about your own progress. If you must compare with someone else, compete with the runner you were last week. That is a much better race to be in and it is a fair competition.

- **SMILE:** Even if you don't feel like smiling, give it a try. It will help you relax, as well as feel taller and more positive. Remember how lucky you are to be able to get out there and run, and be grateful for this. No one is making you do it – you are lucky to be able to do it. Enjoy it.

- **ENJOY IT:** If running is not enjoyable, you will very quickly start making excuses to skip training sessions. The tips above go a long way to increasing your enjoyment levels, but also consider your running route, the time of the day and your energy levels. You will work out in time what suits your body best and then go with that routine rather than feel you have to run at a time and a place that doesn't work for your lifestyle. Notice what you enjoy about running and build more of that into your training sessions.

Beginners' Plan

This programme will guide, support and motivate you through the next eight weeks, building up from walking to running. By the end of the programme you will be able to take on your first 5k. Each training session is made up of thirty minutes of walking and running. In the early weeks there is a lot of walking, but as the weeks go on we gradually replace the walking with running. We are aiming for three training sessions per week, ideally spread out across the week.

FOUR SIMPLE STEPS: From the start I encourage you to get into a routine of warming up, cooling down and keeping track of your progress. Think of your run as being just one part of these four steps: if you get into the routine of organising your runs like this, your future running self will be very thankful.

1. Warm up.
2. Walk/run.
3. Cool down.
4. Write it down (keep track of your progress).

WARM UP AND COOL DOWN: You don't need any fancy routines right now. Simply walk for five minutes either side of your run. You can add in some stretches at the end of your run as the weeks progress (see page 172 for stretching tips). Try not to cut corners on your warm up though, as this will make you feel much stiffer and tighter when you do run.

PLAN TOO HARD? There are no set rules to this plan. If it works for you to take longer walking breaks, please do so. Slow down your pace and repeat any training session or week if you feel it is too hard. You don't have to take eight weeks to get to thirty minutes. Take as long as feels right for you. We all have days (or weeks) where life takes over and we realise that our running has taken a back seat. Rather than give up, just start over or slot back in where you left off.

Mary's beginners' running plan:
zero to thirty minutes in eight weeks

	Mon or Tues	Wed or Thurs	Weekend
Week 1	Run 1 min, walk 2 mins (x 10)	Run 1 min, walk 1 min (x 15)	Run 2 mins, walk 1 min (x 10)
Week 2	Run 3 mins, walk 3 mins (x 5)	Run 3 mins, walk 2 mins (x 6)	Run 4 mins, walk 2 mins (x 5)
Week 3	Run 5 mins, walk 1 min (x 5)	Run 7 mins, walk 3 mins (x 3)	Run 8 mins, walk 2 mins (x 3)
Week 4	Run 8 mins, walk 2 mins (x 3)	Run 9 mins, walk 1 min (x 3)	Run 10 mins, walk 6 mins, run 14 mins
Week 5	Run 11 mins, walk 4 mins (x 2)	Run 9 mins, walk 1 min (x 3)	Run 10 mins, walk 5 mins, run 15 mins
Week 6	Run 12 mins, walk 3 mins (x 2)	Run 9 mins, walk 1 min (x 3)	Run 5 mins, walk 5 mins, run 20 mins
Week 7	Run 13 mins, walk 2 mins (x 2)	Run 9 mins, walk 1 min (x 3)	Run 2 mins, walk 3 mins, run 25 mins
Week 8	Run 14 mins, walk 1 min (x 2)	Run 9 mins, walk 1 min (x 3)	Run 30 mins with a smile!

Frequently Asked Newbie Questions

At this stage I can pretty much predict the questions that the new runners are going to ask me when they attend their first classes. Sometimes I even get the questions asked in advance of class as they feel a little uncomfortable not knowing the basics. It's okay not to know the basics. A coach is there to answer them for you.

What should I wear?

You can spend a fortune on running clothing, or you can keep it nice and simple. For these first eight weeks of your running, comfort is the main priority.

Make sure you are visible if you are running in the dark by wearing a hi-vis vest. If your running wardrobe is non-existent that's fine. Wear what you would wear if you were going for a brisk walk. The only purchase I would highly recommend at this stage is a high-impact sports bra for women. The larger your chest the more you will benefit from the support of the bra. It will take pressure off your back and help your running posture. (Read more about running gear on page 62.)

What about running shoes?

Much like the running clothing, give your running 'career' a few weeks in your existing walking/running shoes until you notice how running feels on your body. If you have not had any problems, continue in your current shoes for these initial weeks and once you have truly caught the running bug treat yourself to a good pair. If you do feel aches and pains in your legs or feel like your existing shoes are heavy, worn out or just too old, bring them along with you when buying new shoes and the sales assistant will be able to see how you move and what type of shoe would be best for your body (see also page 60).

I can't breathe *and* run

Possibly the most common question I am asked by the new runner relates
to breathing. All runners need to be able to multitask breathing and running,
and discomfort when breathing is the primary reason many new runners
give up so soon. Every runner will be out of breath at a certain pace. As a
beginner you need to run at a pace where you can comfortably relax and
talk. There are plenty more days for going faster but please slow down to a
pace where you don't feel out of breath. It doesn't matter if walkers overtake
you. The slower you go, the better in these early days until your body
becomes accustomed to running. You can also make your breathing easier
by looking forward rather than down when you run (see page 139). Lengthen
up tall and notice how you can get more air in with each breath.

What will the neighbours think?

I know many new runners who will drive to another part of town to run in
order to avoid anyone they know seeing them out on the streets. Being
self-conscious is very normal, especially if you have not participated in sport
as an adult or are uncomfortable with your body shape or fitness. The truth
is that most people won't even notice you. You are just another runner to
them. If you are concerned about your pace or how red your face night
be, remind yourself that no one you meet knows how long you have been
running for. You could be finishing up a marathon training session of a few
hours, hence your red face and snail's pace. Let them think that if it makes
you feel better. They will never know that this is your first few minutes. Don't
waste any energy wondering what the neighbours or strangers think of you.
Save that energy for the run.

I can't get myself out the door

I totally get this. Motivation is hard, and we all have days where we will
choose even housework over a run. The trick is to find something that will
make you get out the door. We are all so good at making excuses; there
will always be something else more useful that you 'could' be doing instead
of the running. But I can promise you that the feeling you'll get of being
annoyed with yourself for not going is not worth it. You are also significantly
more likely to make an excuse the next time too if you skip today's run.

The four best motivators for new runners are:

1 Going with someone else – when you have a prearranged time to meet someone, you will make it your business to be there.

2 Getting dressed in your running gear – you are far more likely to go out if you feel like a runner.

3 Trying a new route – if you run somewhere different or even reverse the route you normally do, it will seem fresher.

4 Telling someone – it's handy to have someone else warned to push you out the door when you start making excuses.

I don't believe I can do it

After years of believing you are not a runner it's understandable that negative voices come into your head on the run. As the numbers get bigger on your minutes spent running, it can all seem a bit overwhelming. As soon as you start to feel doubts coming in, slow down your pace, smile, relax a little and say to yourself 'I just need to get through this minute and I'll feel better'. By the time you get to the end of that minute it's very likely you will be back feeling strong: stay positive in your head, and your legs will follow.

I like to break up my run mentally into small chunks. I feel it's easier to run three sets of five minutes than a chunk of fifteen minutes. Try running the first five minutes, mentally discard those five minutes and tell yourself you are now out for a ten-minute run. Keep discarding the minutes until you are down to a few minutes, which you know you can do. It's all about tricking your head into making the run seem manageable.

Where should I run?

A grass or woodland trail is ideal running terrain, but when starting out it's good to be practical too. If you are short on time you can indeed run right from your front door (once you have warmed up). Keep in mind, though, that paths and roads are harder on the body so if and when you do get a chance to run on grass, sand or a lovely path through the woods, do take it. In terms of safety, only run where you would feel comfortable walking alone. Be mindful of uneven surfaces, footpaths on a slope and of course the lovely weather features of ice or wet leaves which can be slippery. Personally, I would avoid a treadmill if I could. It's not bad for your body but it's so much better to get the fresh air into your lungs and explore your neighbourhood instead of getting hot and sweaty while watching every second pass by painfully slowly on the screen in front of you.

Should running be painful?

In a word, no. It's only normal that you may feel slight aches or discomfort when you start out running, but not real pain. Your body will adapt gradually, and most of the beginners' aches and pains disappear over the first few weeks. You have to become the judge of your body yourself and notice how it is feeling. Don't run through pain. Slow down to a walk, relax your body and try

again. Be conscious of your warm up and your pace. They are the primary cause of pains in beginner runners. Try getting off the paths and roads for a softer surface and take a look at your shoes: they may need an upgrade. Be sure to spend five to ten minutes cooling down after your training session. Many people find a nice hot bath a good thing to loosen out the muscles after a run. Good technique helps enormously: you will hear plenty more about that in the coming chapters.

How do I keep track of the minutes?

In the initial stages of running there can be a lot of clock-watching as we alternate between walking and running. Rather than have your head in a watch for your first month of running, consider downloading a free app on your phone which you can programme to beep when you should start and stop running. There are lots of 'interval timer' apps out there – listen out for the beep which will guide you as you alternate between walking and running. You'll need to use something to carry your phone so you're not holding it in your hand all the time though – a running belt or armband, readily available, are just the job for this. A less technical alternative is a friend who runs/cycles alongside you with the job of being the clock-watcher. You decide which might work best for you.

How can I track my distance?

Most new runners are keen to know the distance they have travelled and how long they have been running. As a beginner you won't be out on the road too long so starting out with a phone app is a good way to go before you invest in any big gadgets. Long-standing running apps such as Runkeeper and MapMyRun are used by many runners because they track the running metrics such as pace, distance and route using the GPS in your phone to give you real-time updates on your run and allow you to view your training afterwards.

Once you get into the running routine you will discover more popular apps such as Strava for runners, but let's keep it simple for now. Do notice if any of the apps impact your battery. With GPS and the apps constantly looking for your location some can hit your battery power. A phone app is no good if the second half of your run is not recorded because your battery is dead. This is the reason why many long-distance runners eventually use a running watch to record their running statistics. You don't need to ever look at a watch or a phone if that doesn't motivate you, but I know most of you secretly love to see where you have travelled and how long it took to get there.

What gadgets do I need?

Gadgets are not essential – if you just want to run free and don't have the interest in (or patience for) statistics, that's perfectly fine. For those who love gadgets, though, there's a huge array of running watches out there, varying from quite basic to ones that practically do the run for you. If Christmas or your birthday is coming up, drop a few hints. I would suggest you choose one that can tell you at the very least your distance travelled, your current pace, the pace of your last kilometre and the time you have been on your feet. I have had some of the fanciest watches but generally have only looked at this type of basic information when on the run. Most of our gang have chosen the Garmin brand.

Find Your Perfect Shoe

I'm often asked what running shoes I wear or what running shoes are the best. The answer to both of those questions is not straightforward. Simply put, there are no 'best' running shoes. There are just the 'best shoes for your feet'. We are all different in our makeup and feet biomechanics and need different levels of support and structure to support our running body.

I certainly own more running shoes than 'proper shoes'. I have the good pairs, the long-distance ones, the 'wear on the beach' shoes, my favourite old pair, the light barefoot ones, the chunkier trail ones, the brightly coloured speed shoes and the few pairs that I took a chance on buying online but that never quite fitted right. Some I wear regularly while others have long since served their time. There is a selection of brands, styles and sizes. My years of being loyal to one shoe type are long gone.

I would always recommend a trip to your local independent running specialist shop if you need help in selecting new running shoes. The staff in these shops are passionate about running and are trained to know the mechanics of feet and how we move when running. Bring your current running shoes and they will check how you have worn them down. The best running specialist shops will be confident enough in their advice to let you take the shoes home, try them indoors and decide if they are right for you. It may be tempting to buy online or from a generic sports outlet but until you know exactly what your feet need, get practical expert advice.

The lifetime of your shoes really depends on your mileage, how well you look after them and a little bit of luck. The sellers of running shoes recommend you replace them every eight hundred kilometres or six months, depending on use. Over time the shoes lose their support through wear and tear and don't offer the same level of protection as new shoes. All the kilometres add up, so if you are walking to work in them every day you are reducing their lifespan. If you know you love a pair, try and get a replacement sooner than later – like any fashion, the styles and fits change each season.

For long-distance runners it is nice to have two 'active' pairs of identical runners in your wardrobe – one pair that you love for the long runs and a 'weekday' pair that gets you through the shorter ones. It means that your long-run shoes are reasonably fresh for your race day and both sets of shoes get a break at some stage. Try to organise your running shoes so that all pairs don't need replacing at the same time. It's helpful to have one new pair settling in as another is reaching the end of its life.

When you come to buy your running shoes, don't judge by the brand or the price; go with what feels right for you. Running shoes are a big investment but in the long run (pun not intended), looking after your feet correctly will save you on medical bills. No matter how good your technique is, we all have different foot sizes, shapes and running history behind us. Don't get taken in by any fads and remember that your foot does need to be able to move its component parts while in a shoe so always check there is good flexibility in the sole. Try not to pick based on the colour. Inevitably the ones that are least attractive on the eye are the ones that fit the best.

We have all bought high heels which look fabulous but after a night out have damaged our feet, toes and our comfort. Don't do the same with your running shoes. A good pair will make you want to put them on. A bad pair, or a worn-out pair, will leave you cursing them, just like those dodgy high heels. If you are feeling guilty about splashing out so much on a sports item, think about how many items you have in your wardrobe that you have only worn a few times. I like to justify my running shoe habit by considering a cost-per-wear benefit. When I am questioned as to why I'm buying yet more I explain that technically they are costing practically nothing when you distribute the cost across the many days they will be worn.

Oh, What to Wear?

Once you have the shoes sorted, you still need to figure out what to wear. I'm really not the best person to tell you what you should wear, as I stick to very simple basics of black bottoms, a sports bra and my Running Chick breathable T-shirts. I'm not as fashion-conscious a runner as maybe I could be. But I am comfortable in what I wear and that is the most important thing. Have you ever worn that old pair of running pants that has the stretched elastic that keeps falling down? Or the pair of socks that keep slipping underfoot? Maybe you have spent half a run carrying a heavy jacket as you baked in the heat. We have all made fashion mistakes in running, but we generally don't make the same mistake twice.

When it comes to running clothing you don't need too many layers and certainly not any heavy layers. You will warm up and being able to tie a loose layer around your waist is a lot easier than having to carry it around under your arm when you get too hot. When you find a pair of socks that works for you, go and buy a few more pairs. Make sure you have somewhere to carry your keys and your phone, and after that just be guided by what feels right for you.

Certain accessories I deem essential: a slather of sun cream even on days when you don't think it's that warm, a hat and gloves in the winter that you can stick into your leggings once you get warmer and a good-quality supportive sports bra for women. Reflective gear is incredibly important for running when the days and nights are dark. Everything else is an individual choice. Thankfully once you become a runner you'll find that people only buy you running stuff for presents and gifts. Make sure you get the gear you want by dropping a few not-so-subtle hints coming up to gift-giving times.

Get It Right From the Start

In a nutshell these are the habits that work for most new runners:

- Following a clear plan.

- Training three times per week.

- Spreading out rest days during the week.

- Focusing only on the current week.

- Having a set time of the day to run.

- Engaging friend/family support.

- Warming up and cooling down.

- Keeping the pace slow.

- Writing down progress.

- Being patient.

Futureproof Your Running Body

If you are serious about running becoming a long-term hobby, it is important to look after your body and stay motivated. I encourage all runners to focus on the following areas as they increase their running minutes.

LEARN TECHNIQUE: A lot of runners place huge pressure on their lower legs and hips when running. I coach Chi Running Technique to all beginners to help them learn good technique from the start and will share with you some of the technique tips later in the book. It is a lot easier to learn right from the start than change a bad habit (see Chapter 7).

GET STRONG: You don't need to start heavy weightlifting. Even a few minutes of strength work at home each day can help your body feel more capable and reduce the load on smaller muscles. Build a few strength exercises into your running routine to help protect your body or consider a Pilates or strength class tailored for runners (see Chapter 7).

BE FLEXIBLE: Keeping the body mobile and flexible is key to lifelong running. I like to start all training sessions with a mobilising warm up and finish the run with a cool down walk and a series of full body stretches to loosen out the muscles which have worked hard during the run. Some runners love yoga stretches and over time you will identify what muscles you need to work on most (see Chapter 7).

KEEP A RUNNING DIARY: Make the time to keep a journal of your progress. Whether it's a short scribble or a detailed story make it clear enough to easily remind you of any points worth remembering. Your early weeks of running will soon start to blur so it's great to capture the feelings you have now so you can look back over this in the future for affirmation of how much you improved over time (see Chapter 5).

The First Eight Weeks

On the first day of week one of my beginners' classes everyone has a nervous laugh when I tell them that running for thirty minutes in eight weeks' time will be no problem to them. Most are just anxious about fitting in or being left behind. They generally don't believe it is possible for them to be a runner. But the time flies by as they chat and go through the stages with their running buddies. Before they know it I'm announcing it's time to stop running. 'Graduation night' is one of my favourite times to be a running coach and it's an emotional night for everyone. I'm mindful of so many of the background stories of the students and all they have overcome to get here.

Moving from walking to be able to run for thirty minutes is one of the biggest running achievements there is out there. You go from not being a runner to being a runner. After that running is all about new challenges and increments in speed or distance. Whether you are training in a group or alone, thirty minutes is a wonderful achievement and a stepping stone for wherever you wish running to take you. Once you get to the end of the programme I promise you will be a different person. Gone will be the individual who was full of insecurities about their own running potential and instead there will be a positive, enthusiastic runner who now regrets not starting sooner. With the whole world of running on your doorstep, this new you has now got a new hobby, better fitness but, most important, a whole new attitude towards running and towards life. The change in mindset is worth more than any change in fitness. Knowing that you have committed to something for eight weeks and have seen such changes in your body (and head) shows you that if you can do this, you can do anything.

Your First 5k Event

When you can run thirty minutes non-stop, at no matter what pace, you are ready for the big one. Your first official 5k. Indeed, you may still feel the doubts creep back in when you imagine a large group of runners lined up at a start line, but I guarantee that once you get moving all that will be forgotten. For many first-time 5k runners you will be probably on your feet between thirty and forty minutes. It is a lot different when you are in a group than alone – you just won't give up five minutes from the end. The energy of the event will carry you through.

I still remember my first 5k and have had the honour of being at the finish line of many of my students' first 5k. It's emotional, empowering and exciting. You only get one first 5k so enjoying it is essential. If you are keen to have a race number on your T-shirt and a big fanfare for your first 5k, check out local events organised by running clubs and charity races or make a weekend of it and travel somewhere else. The key will be finding an event that suits your schedule. Ideally take part in the 5k within a few weeks of running your first thirty minutes. This is the perfect timing to keep you motivated and take advantage of all you have achieved by starting your running journey. (For race day jitters see Chapter 8.)

BE WARNED ... After doing a race you will want to book the next one. The adrenaline is flowing, and you feel like you could run a marathon (please don't sign up for a marathon for at least another year or two). I recommend that anyone starting out continues to enjoy the 5k distance for at least a few months before going any longer in distance. You can challenge yourself to get stronger and faster over 5k but don't rush into longer distances too soon. You have the whole rest of your life to run for longer so don't hit all the milestones too quickly or you will have nothing to look forward to.

Tips for your first 5k

1 BE PREPARED – PACK THE NIGHT BEFORE Make a list of everything you need to bring and set it all out the night before the race. Avoid any last-minute panics by being prepared, so you don't have to think on race morning (see page 184).

2 DRESS FOR THE OCCASION Wear whatever clothes you would normally wear when running. Don't try anything new on the day. If you do, you may suffer from chafing or blisters and that would take the fun out of such a great occasion. If the weather is cool, bring an old jumper/fleece that you can discard at the start line and not be too concerned if it's not there when you return. Also, if it is raining, bring a large black sack which you can wear over your body to avoid getting soaked. Once again, remove it just at the start.

3 ARRIVE EARLY Give yourself plenty time to prepare for the race. I recommend you arrive one hour before start time. This gives plenty of time for collecting your race number, doing multiple toilet trips, warming up and soaking up the atmosphere. The last thing you want to be is tired from having to race to the start line!

4 PLAN YOUR FOOD AND DRINK In the two days before your race, avoid alcohol, drink plenty of water and eat good healthy food. For 5k (and even 10k), if you are well hydrated in the days leading up to the race, you should not need to drink lots of water on race morning. If you drink too close to the race, you will spend the warm-up time queuing for smelly portaloos. Have a light version of your normal breakfast at least two hours before the race (most runs start in the morning). You won't be hungry when running! Bring a bottle of water with you to the race, just in case. You can always drink it afterwards.

5 DON'T PANIC There will always be people who are faster, stronger, more athletic-looking than you. Don't compare yourself to them. You are running your own race. Your target is to reach your goal – not their goal. You have no idea how long they have been running. Don't compare yourself to them. You are well prepared. Remember the runner you were eight weeks ago, relax, enjoy the start line atmosphere and try to keep calm.

6 PACE YOURSELF With all the excitement at the start line, many people get carried away with pace and start running too fast. If you start too fast, you will struggle towards the end. Learn to pace yourself from the start. If you start towards the back of the group, you are more likely to avoid taking off with the leaders.

7 BRING SOME CHEERLEADERS Having friends or family along the route can be a great motivator. Not only will they be able to mind your bags when you are running, an encouraging cheer along the route will keep you smiling, positive and focused. Let your cheerleaders know what a big deal this race is for you and be sure to give them a wave and smile as you run past them, head held high!

8 STAY POSITIVE There may be times during the race when you feel like walking, quitting running forver or even crying. Try to remember all the effort you have put in to be here, and how easy it would be not to do this race. Picture yourself finishing the race strong and how you will feel when you cross the finish line. Slow down if you need to, catch your breath, refocus and remember what an achievement it will be to complete it. You can only do your best. Keep focused on your race.

9 FINISH WITH A SMILE AND SPRINT As soon as you are close to the finish line, put on your biggest smile, fix your posture, feel strong and keep your eye on the finish. Feel yourself being drawn towards that line. Picture yourself being as strong as you can and enjoy the cheers and clapping as you make your way up the finishing stretch. You will get a second wind, no matter how tough you have found the race. Prepare to feel a little emotional too.

10 CAPTURE THE MOMENT Congratulations – you did it. Now don't forget what a big deal it is, and how you felt on the day. Ideally write down everything about the day and store it away as a motivating read for your next race. In years to come, you will look back on that race with fond memories. If you can't face writing your story, at least take a photo to help you remember the achievement.
You only have one first race – make it one to remember.

Try parkrun

If you cannot find an official 5k race locally, or don't really want to invest in one, there is another alternative which is on every week and is 100 per cent free. As the name suggests, 'parkrun' is a Saturday morning 5k event in various parks all around the country and across the world and it's the best thing to hit running in a very long time.

I love parkrun. As a runner, a coach, a volunteer or even just a Facebook follower, parkrun works. As you know by now, although I'm a running coach, I don't always have that morning enthusiasm to go running. I am the same as many others. I make excuses and I invent chores to put off my run. I am an expert at talking myself out of running. Even when I do manage to go for a run, I am too nice to myself; I run at a comfortable pace, I take shortcuts, I avoid hills. I somehow just can't get myself to push out a fast (well fast for me) 5k on my own.

But parkrun does all the hard work for me:
- It gets me up out of bed and at a start line at 9.30 a.m. No excuses.
- I can arrive at 9.15 a.m., warm up en route, jog to the start line and get going. No hanging about.
- I will always push myself more in a parkrun than on my own.
- It has an addictive quality of making me want to beat my own PB.
- It is social, welcoming, and relaxed – and most of all FREE!
- It is always followed by a reward – a cuppa and a chat with other runners.
- It's the same run each week, so I compare my times week on week.
- Apart from running, I can always volunteer and still be part of it all.
- Best of all, it gives me that lovely smug post-run feeling at 10 a.m. on a Saturday morning that sets me up for the weekend.

At the end of each of our class terms I encourage the group to go together to a parkrun to support our first-time parkrunners. If parkrun can feel accessible and welcoming, which it is, then people are more likely to return on their own. Friendships have been made as runners meet the same faces each week. They enjoy the pre-run banter, the mid-run encouragement and the post-run debrief and shared breath-catching recovery camaraderie. Many of these runners will happily admit they wouldn't bother getting up for a run on their own, but there is something about parkrun that gets them out of bed.

Parkrun is growing at such a rate that there seem to be new venues every week. It's volunteer-based so we all chip in to help out but we all get back so much more than we put in. If you are intimidated about a group environment, go down one morning, pretend you are out for a walk and just observe. While not everyone has the benefit of being able to train midweek with a group, there is a running crew ready to support you on Saturday morning if you can just get yourself up and out. There are hundreds of success stories from parkrun. It offers what I believe is what will keep us all running going forward – a running community, partners in crime and people who understand you but are not in competition with you.

Keeping the Momentum Going

After the initial momentum and enthusiasm of your first eight weeks and your first 5k event you may find that it is harder to keep yourself motivated without a set plan and without running the longest run of your life every week. We all need something to keep ourselves going. As much as we enjoy running, we all have days where motivation is not what it could be and missing one run can lead to missing a week or two. Before we know it we have lost the routine. Slowly after we lose the routine we then lose the confidence and the fitness, and it becomes harder to get going again.

Continue to get out the door three times per week. Not every run needs to be 5k but aim for that once per week to keep the momentum up – the 5k distance has a lot going for it:

- It is short enough to take minutes rather than hours.
- You generally don't need to carry water or food.
- You can sneak it in at lunchtime or before work.
- You can challenge yourself over the distance if you wish or take a more leisurely pace to enjoy a new route or scenery.

If you know you might struggle, try one of my motivation tips (see Chapter 5). If you liked having a plan as a beginner, here is the next level. It's just four weeks but you can repeat it as many times as you like. Each time you repeat it you get stronger.

Mary's keep it going plan

	Mon or Tues	Wed or Thurs	Weekend
Week 1	A leisurely 3–5k enjoying the fresh air and freedom.	30 mins – run slowly for 15, turn around and run faster home.	5k – time yourself or do a parkrun.
Week 2	A leisurely 3–5k enjoying the fresh air and freedom.	4km with a few hills along the way.	5k with no pressure on speed.
Week 3	A leisurely 3–5k enjoying the fresh air and freedom.	30 mins – run slowly for 15, turn around and run faster home.	5k with no pressure on speed.
Week 4	A leisurely 3–5k enjoying the fresh air and freedom.	4km with a few hills along the way.	5k or parkrun same route as Week 1 – how does it feel?

EVERY RUN: Start out with five minutes warmup and finish with five to ten minutes cooldown and stretches/mobility work.

Moving Up the Kilometres

As you become more confident over the 5k distance you might get itchy feet and consider going a little longer. Just because you hear of people running 10ks, half marathons or even marathons doesn't mean you have to do them right now. Yes, they may be in your future, but isn't it great to have something to look forward to rather than rushing to achieve everything now and risking losing the attraction of running you have worked so hard to find?

Take your time in building your distance if you do have your eye on the long road. If you enjoy running you will be more likely to stay running long-term so make that the priority now rather than setting too many long-distance goals. We all will take different running paths, but consider some of the following a sensible approach.

- **YEAR 1:** Build to 5k and enjoy it. Maybe consider training for 10k after six months if you feel the urge.
- **YEAR 2:** Stay over 5k and/or 10k and get stronger, faster and more comfortable.
- **YEAR 3:** Consider long distance by gradually moving to a half marathon before committing to a marathon. Or just stay happily at 5k and 10k and continue to love how running makes you feel.

I know some of you reading this have no intention of taking so much time to gradually build the distance running goals. If you do have a dose of 'runner's impatience' and want to run long before your body has got accustomed to running, please do listen to your body, make sure to protect it from the road and the additional mileage (see Chapter 9).

From 5k to 10k

Eight weeks can take you from 5k to 10k once you are completely comfortable with your 5k. The only change from your regular maintenance training plan is that your weekend run gets longer each week. The rest remains the same, so why not give it a go if you need a new challenge? If you are training for your first 10k, don't get caught up on speed. Aim to finish each run comfortably. You have plenty of time to get faster over 10k once you have completed your first one.

Mary's 5k to 10k training plan

	Mon or Tues	Wed or Thurs	Weekend
Week 1	A leisurely 5k enjoying the fresh air and freedom	30 mins – run slowly for 15, turn around and run faster home.	5.5km run
Week 2	A leisurely 5k enjoying the fresh air and freedom.	4km with a few hills along the way.	6km run
Week 3	A leisurely 5k enjoying the fresh air and freedom.	30 mins – run slowly for 15, turn around and run faster home.	6.5km run
Week 4	A leisurely 5k enjoying the fresh air and freedom.	4km with a few hills along the way.	7km run
Week 5	A leisurely 5k enjoying the fresh air and freedom.	30 mins – run slowly for 15, turn around and run faster home.	8km run
Week 6	A leisurely 5k enjoying the fresh air and freedom.	4km with a few hills along the way.	8.5km run
Week 7	A leisurely 5k enjoying the fresh air and freedom.	30 mins – run slowly for 15, turn around and run faster home.	9km run
Week 8	A leisurely 5k enjoying the fresh air and freedom.	4km with a few hills along the way.	10km run

Chasing the Clock

Running your lifetime fastest time over a certain distance is incredibly empowering: the feeling you get when you cross the finish line is the reason so many of us keep on running. The chase for this elusive personal best tempts runners from the elite to the novice. In fact, some runners measure their running success entirely based on this number. Although rewarding when it all goes to plan, the stress and pressure to hit a time target can be frustrating and challenging.

When starting out running the constant achievement of gradual speed improvements is empowering and exciting. Consider the 5k distance. For a beginner, they enjoy the buzz of hitting a PB quite regularly. As the body adapts to running and both strength and confidence increase, the runner can comfortably improve their time consistently in the first year of running. Without any specific speed training, the PBs become a welcome reward and motivator for the new runner.

As the months and years progress personal bests are harder to come by without significant effort. Fitness and pace start to plateau and breaking through the PB barrier is not as simple as keeping up a regular running routine. As the quick wins of the early days decrease many runners can become frustrated with their lack of progress.

We cannot expect the body to continually get faster if we don't challenge it and adapt our training. It doesn't come easy. You have to work for it.

Getting Faster

We all have the potential to run faster if we put the work in and are willing to endure a little more discomfort in our training. Introducing a little speed training to our week can help runners get stronger, more confident and faster overall. If all the kilometres we run during the week are at the same pace our bodies will struggle to run quicker when we call on them to perform on a race day. We need to add some variety to our pace in training if we want to become faster runners.

Fear of speed

Speed training can sound intimidating for a newbie, conjuring up visions of endless laps of a track run at a vomit-inducing pace. If you search online for speed training tips, you may be baffled by the terminology. Having to measure distance, heart rates, recovery times and repetitions can sound so complicated that it may prevent you getting started. Try not to get overwhelmed by complex training sessions or attempting to train like an Olympic athlete. Instead, as with any good practice, ease into speed work gradually. Over time you will build resilience, speed and a knowledge of how much to push yourself. One speed session per week is enough for any recreational runner if you work hard and recover well. Give yourself a rest day each side of this session and continue your running week as normal.

Before you start

Find an area that is bright and obstacle-free. You don't want to spend your run looking down to avoid tripping. Having a clear path for speed work allows you to relax and focus on the task at hand. If you have a track nearby, that is ideal, otherwise find a well-lit area that you are comfortable with.

Be cautious rather than reckless in these early sessions until you know your capabilities. It will take you a few attempts to work out your 'fast' pace as you need to find a pace you can sustain for the duration of the interval.

Here are three simple yet effective speed sessions that you can try out.

- **ONE-MINUTE INTERVALS:** After ten minutes of easy running warm up, spend the next ten to twenty minutes alternating between one fast minute and one slow minute. Your fast pace is not a sprint but fast enough that you can sustain it for the minute and are extremely looking forward to your slow relaxed jog for the recovery minute. Feel free to take a longer recovery if needed between speed intervals as you work out your pacing. Finish this session with an easy ten-minute cool down.

- **HILL INTERVALS:** Often recommended as one of the best types of speed session for runners, hill intervals are exactly what you might expect. You run strong up the hill and then recover slowly on the way back down. Find a gradual incline that takes anything from thirty seconds to a minute to climb. As with the training session on the flat, make sure you're well warmed up before you start, and finish with a gradual cool down. Begin with six repetitions and increase as the weeks go on. Over time you can find longer and steeper hills if you wish to step up the challenge.

- **LONGER INTERVALS:** Longer intervals are hugely beneficial for those training for longer distance events. You will also be training your mental strength to silence the negative voices that shout at you to stop. Running fast for five minutes or longer may sound like torture but remember the pace is not as fast as the previous speed sessions I have suggested. The longer the interval, the more you need to focus on sustaining a manageable pace from the start. Aim to alternate between five minutes slow and five minutes faster over a thirty- or forty-minute run.

Speedy Reminders

Try to relax your shoulders when you do speed work. Tension in the neck and shoulders transfers downwards and limits your potential to run faster and breathe well.

If you find it hard to run through discomfort in your legs and lungs, try organising speed sessions with a running buddy or a group. You don't need to be running at the same pace as the other runner – follow each other's footsteps as you go up and down the same path. The camaraderie will keep you on track and you are less likely to talk yourself into reducing the number of intervals or intensity as the session progresses, which I know from personal experience is very easy to do when training alone. It is hard to get started, but like any good training session, you feel proud, exhilarated and powerful afterwards.

No matter how often you do speed work, it never gets easier: you just get better and stronger. Your body adapts and you get more comfortable with being uncomfortable. There are endless opportunities for adding in variations and time targets to speed sessions, but start by accomplishing the basics and the rest will follow. Speed work trains the body physically but also mentally to stay focused and build resilience. These training sessions don't take any more time than going for an average 5k run but can really help us to improve not only our speed but our running motivation and confidence.

Whether the interval is as short as two lamp posts or as long as a kilometre, stay focused on the body by training your mind not to wander. Assign yourself a goal for the next interval as you recover from the last. It might be as simple as a smile, a focus on breath or a specific element of running technique.

Always keep in mind that there is more to running than just personal best times. The pressures of focusing too much on PBs can take its toll on runners. If your success as a runner is purely measured by this number, there is constant focus on the clock which can lead to excessive tension in the body and in certain situations can overtrain. Speed doesn't have to bring stress and tension to the body. To be able to run relaxed while fast is essential for injury prevention regardless of whether your PB is fifteen minutes or fifty minutes over 5k.

Celine's story

I was 53 in 2015 when I decided to try to run. My pal Peig had just completed the Couch to 5k programme with a local running club and had run 5k non-stop. I was amazed; 5k, non-stop! In my head I had a couple of stumbling blocks that I needed to overcome before I could start. First off, I was on a mission to lose weight and had great success over the previous year. Second, while I was still focused on losing weight, I wasn't confident about putting myself out there to run in front of others. But I was determined to try.

So I downloaded the NHS Couch to 5k programme to my phone and followed it religiously. I used to leave my house at six in the morning (so that no one would see me) and walk/run around a local running track. What amazed me was that each task I was set by 'Laura' (the voice on the podcast), I was able to do. I was also starting to feel a kind of exhilaration at the end of each session which I loved. A sense of such wellbeing and positivity was hard to ignore but so fantastic to experience.

Just before the end of the eight weeks I heard about parkrun and decided, along with Peig, that we'd try it out once I'd completed the programme. Oh my God! What a morning it was, our first parkrun. We were dizzy with excitement, in awe of all these people turning up to run 5k and now we were going to be part of it. Well we did it, hugged each other and hugged anyone that stood still long enough to let us and went home floating on air. Full of pride, enthusiasm and feeling so positive and so well physically.

Over the following weeks we tested out a number of parkrun venues and it was at the St Anne's parkrun in Raheny that I saw girls with T-shirts and hoodies with 'Forget The Gym' on them. I looked it up on the internet and so began the next chapter of my running story. I joined Forget The Gym. It was wonderful. As well as the running class where I would do exercises and runs that I just would never do on my own, there is friendship and camaraderie with a group of like-minded women that is inspiring and a privilege to be a part of. And so began the elation of a series of 'firsts'. First 5 mile, first trail run, first 10k, first 10 mile, first half marathon, first running holiday!

Over the last three years my confidence around running has grown significantly – assisted in no small way by the godsend who is my running buddy – Peig, my Forget The Gym classes and all of the wonderful and inspiring people I've met and continue to meet through running. Peig and I completed our first Dublin Marathon in October 2017. One of my best days ever – you'll never beat that feeling!

I am grateful for each and every run that I do and hope that I can keep running for a long, long time to come. I have had small injuries and some setbacks but as you do, you pick yourself up, dust yourself off and start all over again. I'm never going to be a fast runner, but I can honestly say that every day I put on my runners and get out the door is a great day.

By the way, my initial fear of running in front of others very quickly disappeared when I realised that other runners are only focused on themselves, keeping going and getting to the end of the run!

4

THE
RUNNING
ROLLERCOASTER

The Grateful Runner

There are two days every year when I make sure that I run. My birthday is followed a few days later by Christmas Day. Regardless of the weather I see these two special days as grateful days, days I choose to run without a watch. I'll wrap up and appreciate that another year has passed, and I can still have the luxury of a magic gift that in thirty minutes lifts stress and worries and generates energy and feel-good endorphins. As a runner, there is so much to be thankful for and so much to look forward to.

We may not be getting any younger or faster, but we have bodies that allow us to reap the mental as well as physical benefits of running. On these landmark runs I reflect on the running year and decide what changes and challenges are right for me next year. I think of the races, the memories and the lessons learnt. I think of the people I have met, the runners I have coached and the new routes and adventures that running has brought to me over the year. Running is indeed the gift that keeps on giving. There is always more to learn, to read and to explore when you are a runner. There are no perfect runners, yet we can always aspire to improve.

Very few of us stay running all the time. Even with the best intentions, it happens. We fall off the running wagon. Before we know it, we are out of the routine, time rolls by and we realise that we haven't run for a while. A sabbatical from running may be intentional due to an injury, illness, pregnancy or life priority changing but most often it can happen by accident. Skipping one run makes the next run easier to miss. The longer the break, the harder the comeback.

Making Time to Run

Let me tell you a secret. You will never have the time to go for a run. There will always be something more urgent to be done. Although running makes us feel so good, we often feel guilty about leaving jobs behind and spending time on something that is just for us and no one else. There are times when it seems impossible to run, but there are windows in every week we could take advantage of if we took the time to see them and not fill them with other jobs. Each day that you skip knocks a little piece off your fitness and your running confidence and makes that future runner you see a little further away.

The trick is to find a way to make running a non-negotiable part of your week. Steal the secrets of dedicated runners. Try to make running an important part of your day rather than an optional luxury for when everything else is done. Carve out a little time in your day for you (see Chapter 5, Motivation Secrets). One point to remember is that your mood determines the atmosphere in your home. When you are happy and content, everyone else benefits. You are calmer, more relaxed and more focused.

Changing Priorities

Even the most dedicated of runners have ups and downs. It's hard to stay going and motivated all the time and it's only right that running is not always our first priority. Sometimes we need to step back from it and realise that we need a break for our minds, our bodies and our long-term love of running. This is okay! Don't make yourself run if you don't want to be a runner right now. Instead, find something that does interest and motivate you. There will be months and maybe years when running is not right for you. If you are in that stage, then accept it and leave your comeback until you are ready.

Throughout my thirties I loved long-distance running. I travelled and ran marathons and ultra marathons throughout Europe and beyond and loved it all. Then one day I realised I wasn't enjoying marathons any more. After forty marathon finish lines the buzz was gone. I took a step back and decided to focus on other elements of running. Rather than just continue to run marathons to add to the numbers I decided that if I was to continue running long distance I needed to let it go for a while. I had become too complacent at the long distance and the novelty had worn off. My body felt fine, but my heart wasn't in it. I needed to reignite my passion for running. I still love the marathon distance and adore coaching and supporting marathon runners and have no doubt that at some point I will return to the long-distance run. For now, I get my marathon buzz from my students, their training runs, their setbacks and achievements and of course their finish line sprints and emotional journeys. But more about marathons in Chapter 9.

Managing Setbacks

Most runners will encounter at least one hiccup which has nothing to do with motivation or prioritising time to run. Injury or illness can strike and send many a well-intended runner off the roads and into a panic. For the dedicated runner this can be seen as a disaster as running plays a huge part in their identity and routine. They will agonise over lost kilometres and deteriorating fitness. Runners sometimes choose to ignore the early warning signs of an injury and continue to run regardless of new aches and pains. I see it often with marathon runners who are so focused on the long run that they neglect their body, fail to listen to warning signals and end up having to take a longer break while everyone around them continues to run.

It is important to take a step back when something like this happens and not rush into a running comeback until your body is ready. It is easy to get anxious and restless and it is why many runners return to the roads too soon and end up regretting it. As a running coach, my job mainly involves reassuring runners to keep calm, make sensible decisions and not let minor setbacks derail their running dream. We need to maintain a level of flexibility in our training and sometimes we just need to make a sensible and brave decision to take a break.

Runners' Guilt

It can be difficult to watch from the side lines as friends and running buddies log kilometres and put photos online. Without running in their lives, runners can find their mood can head in the wrong direction. Yes, you may feel jealous if not resentful of other runners you see out there. But the break from the road doesn't mean it's wasted time as there are lots of things that don't involve just running kilometres. Rather than panicking about what running you are not doing, now is the opportunity to focus on what you have done to date and what other things you can do instead of running that will help your return. A training diary can be a very reassuring read. Without the diary all our good runs and achievements blend into a blur in our memory and it's hard to see beyond the most recent setback.

Think very carefully before you run distances with a body that would benefit more from rest. A short break now to nurse a niggle or fatigue is better than a longer break later in the year to manage an injury that could have been avoided.

You can train your head while the legs take a break. There are many simple but powerful exercises you can do to prepare like an elite athlete, using this time to apply some basic sports psychology to your training. You will calm the nerves, reduce anxiety and build confidence, all without running a minute. From visualisation to positive self-talk, the benefits of mental training cannot be overstated. Removing the worries from your head and putting them on paper will calm the mind (see page 224). You could also use this time to focus on all the other elements of running that you keep putting on the long finger (see Chapter 8). We all know there are things we could do to improve our running off the road. Don't let a setback destroy your belief in your ability. Resting is not cheating. One thing is certain, you will appreciate your running when you cautiously make your comeback.

Barbara's setback and comeback story

I came to running late enough, having never enjoyed it as a child. After a flurry of training for a 10k with a friend (which I enjoyed) I kind of lost my mojo. A year or so later I was bored by my gym classes and I realised that I missed exercising outdoors. So I dusted off my runners and joined Forget The Gym. The running classes introduced me to a large group of women who were all focused on supporting and inspiring each other week after week. So I settled into the group and enjoyed a good running routine for a couple of years, doing weekly classes and some 5k and 10k events.

Then in 2016, I got very ill unexpectedly and ended up having three bowel surgeries over a sixteen-month period. During that time, my body went through a lot of changes and running was not a possibility. However, I had great faith in my surgeon and his confidence that my life would return to normal, so I set myself some goals which included getting back to running. After recovering from my final surgery, I saw a physio for guidance on returning to exercise, thinking I'd be back running in two weeks. But my abdominal muscles had been so seriously weakened that I struggled with the most basic exercises. In the end, I worked with my physio for six months before she was happy for me to start gentle running.

I've been back running for three months now (starting with one minute walk, one minute run) and I can't explain the joy I feel. I'm sure I don't look particularly joyful as I huff and puff towards thirty minutes of running, but the sense of achievement I experience when I reach my target is fantastic. Getting back to my Forget The Gym class in recent weeks feels like the end of my 'illness journey' and the start of normal life again. Over these recent years I have experienced how quickly illness can hit but I have also experienced the body's ability to heal. I am determined to be for ever grateful for good health and hold on to the joy and satisfaction of simply being able to run.

Making a Running Comeback

It's never easy starting back. It's normal to be apprehensive about the first run. We often doubt our ability and our strength to return to former fitness. Certainly, the first few weeks of adapting to your new routine will be less comfortable than when you left off, but postponing the return to running any longer won't help.

Start small, keep it simple and accept that you may find it a challenge from the start. The fitness and confidence will return in time, but only if you give your body and mind a chance to remember how good it feels to be a runner by building slowly, sensibly and gradually over the coming weeks.

Don't get annoyed about the time you have had away from running and the fitness you have lost. Instead, focus on getting started again. The trick is to get out the door and accept that the first five minutes is going to be a challenge. Give yourself the option of going home if you don't start to feel better after those five minutes. Also give yourself the choice to walk as much as you wish. If you can return home knowing you have enjoyed a run/walk you are much more likely to go again. This is how habits are made. It doesn't matter if you walk or run the distance, you will still have benefited from thirty minutes of fresh air and re-established a routine of getting out the door. Each session will get easier from there. The first one back is always the hardest.

How Rusty Are You?

If it has been over a year since your last run or if you have had an injury or illness that has impacted your fitness and mobility a lot, I would recommend you go right back to my eight-week beginners' training plan (see page 50). If, on the other hand, you know there is some fitness in there somewhere and you just need a bit of structure to get back into running, try out this comeback plan which will have you back up to 5k in four weeks.

Repeat any week until you feel comfortable with it, take longer walking breaks, go slower and generally use the plan as a guide rather than a rule. You may choose even to extend it over eight weeks rather than four. Start out with five minutes warming up and finish with five minutes cooling down and stretching.

A comeback can be short-lived if you set your expectations too high. Do not compare with other runners or your previous running times; instead focus on your own body as it is today. Structure is key. Find a friend, a coach or a running buddy to keep you accountable and on a steady track for the first few weeks and months. Don't let the frustration or discomfort of the comeback send you back into another running hiatus. This plan will help bring you back up to 5k gradually and sensibly.

Mary's comeback plan

	Mon or Tues	Wed or Thurs	Weekend
Week 1	3 mins run, 2 mins walk (x 6)	5 mins run, 1 min walk (x 5)	7 mins run, 3 mins walk (x 3)
Week 2	9 mins run, 1 min walk (x 3)	12 mins run, 3 mins walk (x 2)	14 mins run, 1 min walk (x 2)
Week 3	5 mins run, 5 mins walk, 20 mins run	9 mins run, 1 min walk (x 3)	3 mins run, 2 mins walk, 25 mins run
Week 4	30 mins run with two breaks whenever you need them.	30 mins run with as few breaks as you can.	5k or parkrun

5

MOTIVATION SECRETS

I've always been curious as to why some people have no issue with motivation while more of us struggle to get out the door and running. Why do some of us make excuses and postpone something that makes us feel amazing? Why do others run consistently and never procrastinate?

Someone once told me only to study something as an adult that you would happily read a book about in your spare time. Well, I have a library of books on running habits and fitness psychology which I happily read for fun. I decided to delve further into the topic and go back to college to find out more. An MSc in Sports and Exercise Psychology would hopefully teach me the secrets of success and a few mind games to help my runners (and myself) spend less time procrastinating and more time running.

In 2012 I packed my schoolbag and headed up north to the University of Ulster to study. My dissertation looked at the issue I was faced with every day with my running students – motivation, or lack thereof. More than six hundred runners volunteered to take part in my research project which focused on female recreational runners/joggers in Ireland highlighting the difficulties, barriers and obstacles individuals face when maintaining a running routine. To summarise a twelve-thousand-word paper into a few lines, there were two clear differences between the consistent runners and the struggling/lapsed runners.

1. **RUNNING DIARY:** Diaries and training plans were widely used by the consistent runners. Struggling runners were significantly more likely to run only when they 'felt like it' rather than following a structured and planned routine.

2. **RUNNING BUDDY:** Accountability to a 'real person' or the routine of meeting a group/friend for a run was the leading factor that kept runners committed to their running routine.

Turning up consistently is what makes our running blossom and persist right through the good days, bad days and winter days. Maybe I didn't need to ask six hundred people to confirm what I know already works for myself and many of my students, but it is powerful to know that keeping on track is possible with a few simple supports which are all within our control.

The Running Diary

From their very first beginners' running class right up to marathon runners, I ask all my students to keep a training dairy. Those who do keep track only realise its future value when they need a little motivation. It acts as a history of lessons learnt and memories made as well as a planning tool for the dreams ahead.

While we often think of a running diary as being a log of kilometres run, I find it much more useful as a way to track what happened on a given run. While some people keep their notes short, others like to record their memories of the run and anything they might find useful for future runs. We very quickly forget the runner we were last week, so it is lovely to have an opportunity in the future to look back and remember the person we used to be. Below are some steps to make your running diary work.

Choose the right format

Some people like to work off a paper diary, but I prefer an Excel spreadsheet which I can amend or print at any time. There is also the option to use running apps that allow you to add comments to each run as they track your route and distance.

Create a template

Personalise your training plan to fit in with your life. Add your planned training sessions and races to the diary and also 'real life' events such as work or family commitments, so you can picture your future months and recognise where life might take over your running plans.

Update as you go

After every run take one minute to fill in your mini run report. I like to include a line underneath each run and fill in as much detail as I wish. Whether you just want to tick off the run or write an essay is up to you. I know some people like to track the start of a niggle, the impact of a new running terrain, the people they ran with, the music they listened to, the weather or maybe something funny that happened en route. They record their sense of achievement when they finished a good run as well as the upset or disappointment of a run that didn't quite go to plan. Others like to keep it short and sweet with details of the distance and route.

Check in weekly

At the start of the week, take a few minutes to make sure that this week's plan still fits in with your week ahead. Change around sessions if you need to fit your runs around your commitments differently.

Review monthly

Look back over how far you have come and remember the days gone and note the lessons learnt. Add a new month into your template and fill in what you have coming up in the next while so you can plan forward.

Be flexible

Unforeseen events will inevitably occur and impact your plan. From illness to injury, unplanned nights out or family commitments there will be a time where your plan will need to adapt. Being flexible is key. Running should be adding to your life in a positive way, not stressing you out by taking over everything.

Make it yours

Once you get into a routine of doing this you might like to work off an annual sheet. I like to have a new plan for each running year. I include any races or events at the start of the year and highlight in one colour. I highlight any other commitments I have and then as the year goes on it becomes my diary and I get a great view of where I'm going and what I have done. If you like gadgets and statistics, you might like to integrate your diary with your running apps and have all your running history together in one place.

Make it visible

Print out your future plan. Post it on your fridge, your wardrobe, your desk or wherever you know you will see it daily. Keep it in the forefront of your mind and you will never 'forget' to go for a run. Many people enjoy ticking off the sessions as they are completed. Maybe you could invest in some primary school teacher gold star stickers for yourself!

Why Spend the Time Now?

Having a full view of your training on one page will make it clear what has to be done between now and your next goal. It can take the stress out of knowing if you are doing too much or too little. Any new commitments that come your way can be easily added into the plan and you can amend your training to suit these events as they arise. Rather than working towards one big goal way in the future, you can now see the steps and milestones along the way, which makes it more achievable, and this will keep you motivated. There are no rules on how this diary should look.

More than Words

A running diary doesn't have to be just words. Creative runners can doodle, include maps or draw images and charts on paper. Some runners like to see their training plan as a component of a runner's vision board, a place of inspiration for the future. Why not make your running goals and training path more visible by complementing your diary with some running memorabilia and motivation. A printout of your upcoming race route, some photos of the destination, newspaper clippings from last year's event, a few inspiring quotes and even some old race numbers or medals will help build excitement and enthusiasm in your training. Keep a memory box of running memorabilia and look at it regularly, or hang your running inspiration and training plan on a notice board at work or at home. Anything that helps you stay motivated and focused on the goal is worth experimenting with.

The Power of Others

Being part of a running group/club or even having one running buddy can play a huge part in helping you stay committed, motivated and inspired to keep running. Having the regular structure of the meetup adds discipline and routine to running. Some of us never make time for something that's optional and flexible, but if the appointment is made we will turn up. There will be no snooze button on the alarm when we have a friend waiting at the front door at 6 a.m.

Most running buddies don't even start out as friends. They meet in work, at the school gate or at a running group or race event. They start running together for that extra bit of motivation. As the kilometres fly by, they share stories, worries, hopes and dreams that often they may be unwilling to share with even closest friends and family. It might be because there is no eye contact when running that we talk more freely and openly. What is said on the road stays on the road, and we return home both mentally refreshed and pumped with the post-run endorphins. It's no wonder people joke about running being cheaper than therapy.

If the idea of running in a group appeals to you more than running with one person, a running club might be for you. I was always a little intimidated by the thought of joining a running club, assuming it was only for really fast and fit people. While some clubs do focus on their fastest members and define success as speed, there are so many other groups and clubs that have a different ethos.

To be able to combine fitness and friendship is a wonderful gift, so whether you decide to meet with a group, a friend or a colleague for a run, remember you will be helping them just as much as they are helping you. You might even prefer online support. There are plenty of 'virtual' running groups that you can join and feel part of a movement rather than be a solo runner.

'With a running buddy I get exercise and hilarious stories that keep me entertained on the road. It's their great encouragement and shared celebrations and achievements that keeps me running. They are there to say well done and give you a kick/push/poke when you need one too.'
Norma

'My running buddy is the only reason I get up for the early morning runs. I know I wouldn't do it without her.'
Trisha

'Running buddies celebrate the victories (no matter how small) and console you when things don't go to plan. They also know just when to give that vital little piece of encouragement to keep you going.' **Eimear**

'Running buddies are essential for getting you out of bed early on a Saturday and for keeping you sane. Many a fine mile has been run while venting.'
Corinna

'My run buddies have been my therapy sessions over the last couple of months.'
Conor

'I will never win a race, but I will always come back from a run with a smile on my face. I feel very lucky that I have met a great group of running buddies who I also now consider friends with whom I have shared such good times.'
Fiona

Extra Motivation

Even with all the running buddies in the world and a perfect running diary you may still find yourself thinking up excuses. Below are some ideas for wringing out that elusive bit of motivation that you need to leave the house.

- One of our runners, Emma, pops a chicken in the oven and heads out the door. Returning home to the promise of a nice hot shower and the smell of roast chicken keeps her driven to run. Whatever your equivalent of roast chicken is, consider something like this to help you make it out the door.
- Round up a few friends to go away for a day or even a weekend with a run involved. Make it a race distance that is a little challenging. Consider the break away the reward and you will be more inclined to work towards it if you have invested in it. Our annual trip to France in November keeps many a runner in a running routine right through the autumn.
- Get some technical support. Lots of runners love phone apps like Strava as a motivational tool. Tracking statistics of monthly mileage and having targets and mini competitions with friends motivates many runners.
- Consider setting up a WhatsApp group with a few like-minded souls who act as accountability partners. Everyone commits to a certain run and if they are struggling to go, a message of motivation from another points them in the right direction.
- Without a doubt you are more likely to go for a run if you are wearing your running gear. Have all your gear laid out before you go to bed so that you don't have to think in the morning. Avoid opening the curtains before you get dressed. The weather can dictate our willingness to run too, so get dressed and out the door before you decide it's too cold or wet to go out.
- Could your run be part of your commute? If you have no choice but to run, then you will do it. Leave your work clothes in work so the decision is already made. You will get up and go if you have a time deadline.

The First Five Minutes

You are not the only one who struggles at the thought of the start of the run: I know only too well how it feels. Even when I have managed to get myself out, in these first five minutes of a run I can list at least ten reasons why I should go home. I question my potential as I carry my body along the road feeling heavy and lethargic. Then suddenly I feel great. After five minutes there is a switch and I feel like a new person. Running is not that bad after all. The blood is flowing, the body feels looser, the brain relaxes and running actually becomes comfortable.

Never believe what your body tells you in the first five minutes of your run. If you do, you will convince yourself that you are not made for running. The negative voices in your head complain, your breathing can feel laboured, your leg muscles can feel tight and joints might ache. This is normal, especially if you have cut corners in your warm up or have been sitting all day. Thankfully it does pass very quickly – accept that your body just needs a little bit of time to adjust and wake up.

There are people who never get beyond this five-minute barrier because they have convinced themselves that running is meant to be hard work all the time. They start too fast, set unrealistic pace targets and jump straight into a run with a body that is not warmed up. Remember that we are often running after a full day spent sitting down. Take at least five minutes to walk before you run and keep the pace really slow. This will help you hit that positive phase of the run so much sooner.

If you are at home putting off a run reading this, think about a run where you felt good and imagine yourself on that run now. That could be you again if you got up and got out. Go on. You will thank me when you get back.

6

ADD
SOME FUN

Mix It Up

Whether you run alone or in a group you can add some fun to your training. Who says that running has to be a serious hobby? Some runners feel guilty if they stop and walk during a run and put pressure on themselves to run fast and push their body to its limit all the time. Their entire run is spent thinking about getting to the end so they can stop. If the attraction in running is always getting to the end of the run, then why really are we running? I understand and I love the post-run endorphins. Nothing beats the feeling of having a good run completed. But who says we can't enjoy the run as well as the afterparty?

Boredom is a reason why some people lose the love for running. Well, if every run you do is the same route and at the same pace no wonder it becomes monotonous. Over the years I have found that the runs that I really enjoy and that I'm most likely to do again are those that are a little different from my usual 5k route around the block. Building a little variety or a different focus into a run can really make the difference between it being a clock-watching lung-busting workout or an enjoyable, energising training session.

It is not cheating to take breaks along the way of a run. There is no rule to say we have to run non-stop all the time. You can get as good a workout, if not better, by integrating your running with other things, including walks. Fartlek running is a Swedish term for a run that is broken up with different exercises, breaks and paces along the way. We train this way a lot in classes as the runners never know what is coming next and the surprise and the variety keep them guessing and interested. They are only focused on the segment that they are in. Try it on your own, or better still with a running buddy, and take turns at deciding the next exercise or speed interval.

Try Something New

REVERSE YOUR ROUTE: Next time you run, turn the opposite way once you go out the front door. Reverse the usual route and notice how many different things you see. Even a small change like this adds variety and interest to your run. It also helps the body because the gradient on the footpaths and roads is the opposite to normal.

GO OFF-ROAD: Take to the hills or the trails. Pounding concrete pavements can take its toll on the body and running on different surfaces – grass, sand, trail – can make a pleasant change from a footpath. Explore local parks and trails, and see what running off-road does for your focus, concentration, headspace and agility.

TAKE THE BUS: Travel somewhere on public transport. Hop off and run home. The change of scenery and the uncertainly of the route will keep you focused and distracted. Even better, travel a distance you normally travel in your work commute on a run and compare the time it takes.

VARY THE SPEED: If you are new to speed work, be flexible and be guided by your body, not by the clock. You don't have to sprint, just occasionally introduce faster sections followed by slower recovery sections along your route. Run fast when you feel good, then pull back and recover regularly. Over time, your comfortable running pace will get a little quicker and you will enjoy the speed challenge (see pages 79-80 for more speed challenges).

TAKE THE LEAD: Introduce a friend to running. Take the focus off yourself and put your energy into motivating someone else to run. Be the coach with the stopwatch and guide them along an easy walk/run route. The time will fly by and you will remind yourself what running is like for a beginner.

CREATE AN OUTDOOR GYM: Use park benches, steps and walls to build in some mid-run exercises. Try some lunges, step-ups, wall squats, planks and anything you can think of to introduce variety. This is a great session to do with a friend – take turns in deciding what exercise to do next.

TRY A DAWN RUN: Another way to get a new perspective is to run at a different time of day than usual. Morning runners get a different view of the city and countryside before it wakes up. They also have the benefit of having their run ticked off and not having all day to make excuses to put off an evening run. Try a dawn run once and feel smug and energised for the day.

PACK YOUR SUITCASE: As crazy as it sounds, some of the nicest runs can be a little escapism when you are away on your summer holidays. Combined with the early morning start and with the cooler temperatures and quieter paths, you see your destination in a new light. You return to your hotel fresh, energised and ready for a day of holiday fun.

Mindful Running

If you are a slave to running technology or feel like you are losing your running mojo, I challenge you to leave the ego, the watch and the headphones at home and try a little mindful running. Sometimes it's nice to run free. We can often be so focused on the outcome that we forget that we are actually running.

The benefits of mindfulness have been well documented. Decreasing anxiety while helping to improve sleep, mood, creativity, cognitive function, body awareness and general wellness should be enough incentive for anyone to give mindfulness a chance. Being mindful when running is simply a matter of trying to focus on one thing while running, although simple it is not. When running we are often distracted. We think about work, our dinner and to-do list waiting at home. Very often don't think at all about what we are doing at that given moment.

How to run mindfully

Pick one focus from the list below and commit to thinking about it as much as you can on your next run. Don't get frustrated if you find it difficult. It is. When you catch your mind drifting, bring your attention back to that focus and just start over.

- **LOOK:** If you are in the countryside notice how many different flowers you pass by. On a busy road, how many silver cars drive past? In a busy pedestrian area, how many different colour blues do you see on other runners and walkers? Notice how your awareness of your environment improves.

- **LISTEN:** What sounds do you hear on your run? Count them. You will be surprised at how many noises you have not noticed before and how loud they are.

- **BREATHE:** Become aware of your breath. Instead of disguising it by playing your music louder, follow your breath. You might be breathing through nose or mouth, deep into stomach or light into chest and back. Don't try and alter it. Pay attention and follow your breath. Bonus points if you fancy trying breathing in and out of your nose the whole way.

- **THANK:** List everything you are grateful for today that you normally take for granted. Start with all the parts of your body that are functioning properly to help you run today. Move outside your body and be grateful for everything in your environment and everyone who has helped you be where you are today. Use your run as a chance to remember and appreciate them all.

It takes time, effort and a lot of determination to run mindfully so you might not consider it fun at first. It can be harder than pushing your body physically. The ego can kick in and you may be tempted to pick up pace as you see other runners. But go with it and just notice how running feels when distance and speed metrics no longer apply. You might just start to get a lot more out of your running than ever before. Surely that is worth a try.

Combine With Your Passion

When running stops being fun, you risk giving it up. It's up to you to challenge yourself and keep your runs fun and enjoyable. Building variety into your run doesn't have to be just about adding in more exercises, hills or breathing challenges. Could you combine your run with one of your other hobbies or even with your social life?

Organise an event

Rather than meet your friends for Christmas drinks, you could try our favourite Christmas party, the 'Xmas lights run'. We travel around the city taking in all the lights and the atmosphere in the lead up to the big day. Just by chance, we surprisingly happen to finish right beside a Christmas market or a reserved area in a bar with our name on it. It's amazing how runners are drawn towards the smell of mulled wine. It doesn't have to be Christmas to celebrate. Our runners have organised birthday runs, full moon runs and even surprised me with a wonderful hen party run. Running can be a part of any celebration if you take the time to plan it and make it fun.

Volunteer

Rather than focus on your own running all the time, could you give back a little to the community? Consider helping other runners or use your running to raise money for a good cause. Whether this involves volunteering at parkruns or race events, coaching friends or helping out in an athletics club, there are many ways to help other runners. There is even the latest craze of 'plogging' which involves picking up litter as you run so you help save the planet too!

Take some photos

If you enjoy photography, set yourself a challenge to find five good photo opportunities en route. You have my permission to stop and take the snap. It will keep your eyes peeled for what's around you and distract you from looking at your watch. You will notice many things that were there yesterday but never captured your eye.

Be a local tourist

Imagine you are bringing someone on a tour of your neighbourhood and design a route that passes all the highlights. There are roads close to home that you may never have explored, fields and parks on your doorstep that you may never have ventured into and tourist sights and buildings that you may never have even noticed. In Dublin we have created city running tours and also taken the DART on running adventures to scenic seaside suburbs like Dalkey and Howth. It will make you see your locality in a new light. We can all be tourists in our own neighbourhoods.

Create a foodie tour

If anything attracts people to run, it's the promise of something nice to eat at the end. At Forget The Gym we are certainly experts at managing to finish a run close to the promise of food. We choose the parkruns with cafés and food markets, we offered run and cook classes – a run followed by a cookery class – and we have had organised runs to finish at coffee shops, ice cream vans and mulled wine tents. Could you create a little gourmet running route for your friends to follow? I'd certainly be happy to join any running foodie tour I could find.

Travel abroad

I often use running as an excuse to travel and have spent many years researching exotic marathon locations. There is a run everywhere if you look hard enough and it's a fabulous way to meet locals, see the sights and come home with a medal and a suitcase of memories. Today, I'm delighted so many of my running students share the same passion. One of my favourites is our annual trip to Marathon du Beaujolais in France.

Write a blog

Why not consider your run as a source of inspiration if you enjoy putting pen to paper? Anyone can be a running blogger: you only share the stories you want to, and you can write about your running experiences and your progress. For years I kept my Marathon Tourist blog which catalogued my marathon adventures. I wrote it for myself as I knew I couldn't rely on my memory to retain all the wonderful experiences. Even if you don't want to tell the world about your running, a blog becomes a lovely diary to look back over yourself.

Adventures in South Africa:
an entry from my marathon tourist blog, June 2012

Many details I have long forgotten come back to me when I read over some of my blog entries. Here is one of my best memories.

I heard about Comrades a few years ago, and immediately dismissed it as something only crazy people would do. Why would anyone attempt to run almost 90km in African sunshine under the pressure of having to complete it within 12 hours or be disqualified? But here I am. Ready to run.

What a surprise to arrive in Durban, South Africa, to realise Comrades is an institution. Almost 20,000 people had registered for the 2012 Race. Any ultra marathon I have previously completed in Europe has less than 300 taking part! From taxi drivers to shop owners, everyone I met in South Africa has either run the race, watched the 12 hours of TV coverage or wishes to run it one day.

The first Comrades took place in 1921 starting outside the City Hall in Pietermaritzburg with 34 runners. Each year it reverses direction between Pietermaritzburg and Durban, the so-called up and down runs. So, for 2012, I thought I was being smart signing up for what they call the 'Down Run'. In my innocence, I assumed that meant limited uphill and plenty of gentle rolling downhills. I should have read the small print.

The day started with my alarm at 1.30 a.m. By 2 a.m. I was in a taxi with three Brazilians, one other Irish runner (my friend Paul) and a lot of nerves on the 56-mile road to Pietermaritzburg. By 3.20 a.m. we were sitting in a warm café, drinking what was officially called coffee, but not sure what was in the plastic cup. Certainly about four teaspoons of sugar anyhow – well it's all carbs at this stage.

By 4.30am the place started to buzz. Bus loads of runners descended on the town, and the two green Irish tracksuits and freckled skin stood out a mile compared to the locals.

The first hour or so was in the dark. As we left the town of Pietermaritzburg and climbed up, families stood on the side of the road, still in their dressing gowns with cups of tea cheering on the runners. Headphones are banned in South African runs – my first panic, how am I going to run this distance without my motivational music? The only sound was that of the fellow runners pounding the pavement and discussing race strategies. Most people I spoke to had previously run the race. The advice from everyone seemed to be to take it easy for the first half, even if you feel good, as after 70k all sorts of discomfort are to be expected.

South Africans are crazy about rugby. They even know the Irish rugby anthem and all our players' names. The entire route I was serenaded with 'Ireland's Call', 'Say hi to Brian O'Driscoll' and 'What's the craic?' Everyone seemed to be delighted to see an Irish vest.

I have a great ability to forget any pain, hills and discomfort experienced about 24 hours after any long run. Even now, 2 weeks on, I can't seem to remember any discomfort in the race – but I do know it was tough. Why otherwise would it have taken me so long? The route itself, and the order of the various hills, water stations, scenic points and supporter corners are already a distant memory.

In my head, the order of the race went as follows – but I'm certain I'm only remembering a small proportion:
- Climb out of Pietermaritzburg in the dark
- Daylight and seeing the countryside out beyond us
- Being blown away almost with the wind as we climb up to the highest point en route
- The halfway banner and supporters
- The first sight of the sea (finally)
- More uphill than I expected in the second half
- The amazing lap of the stadium at the end

I had trained well (with the exception of serious hill training), so mentally I knew I was capable of the distance. With regard to finishing time, however, I had no idea. I estimated somewhere between 10 and 11 hours, but this was purely a guess. As long as I made it in before the 12-hour gun, I would be happy. That said, it's funny how easy it is to change your time target en route. About 10km into the race, I told myself I would aim for 10 hours 30 mins. About 50k into the race, I revised that to 11 hours. By 80k I knew that wasn't going to happen. Or maybe it could – if my last 10k was faster than any other 10k of the race to date. The odds were against me.

Everyone talks about the supporters at Comrades, and to be honest, I had expected the crowds of a Dublin St Patrick's Day parade with everyone craning necks to see the action. Comrades isn't like that. There were many lonely stretches in quieter country areas and the main supporters were young kids hoping to pick up the discarded running tops and gloves. For the first few hours of the run, I was beginning to doubt the 'atmosphere' of the run. Thankfully all changed, and we moved further into daylight, and towards Durban.

Everyone asks, what do you eat and drink? Do you stop? Where do you go to the toilet? The best question came from my sister who asked if we can stop to go to the toilet, or if you just go while you are running and wash it away with a bottle of water! Thankfully, there are portaloos every few kilometres, and the only problem is that you don't want to get too comfortable or you might lock yourself in there for a bit longer than you might need to. There was plenty of water, energy drinks, biscuits, oranges, and a new one on me – potatoes and salt. As an Irish girl, you would think this would be just the home comfort I needed along the route, but I wasn't able to stomach them.

Once I could see the sea in Durban, I assumed (innocently) it was downhill all the way. With 2 hours to go to get within the 11-hour time limit, surely I could run 18km. My body was feeling fine. In fact some of my fastest kms were in the last 10k, but what disappointment to see more uphills in what I had hoped to be downhill all the way. I think mentally at this point, I lost the 11-hour target – as I knew I would have to slow down on those hills. Everyone said that 70k–89k you have to run with your head as your legs will be shot. Surprisingly my legs were okay, and remained so until the end, just not quick enough to get under the 11-hour gun.

It's hardly the end of the world taking longer than 11 hours, especially as it was a goal I set mid race – but somehow now it has got me. I know I have sub 11 hours in me. I'll just have to go back.

I arrived into the stadium, pacing myself for a full lap, and a large crowd. The crowd was there alright, but actually the lap was much shorter than I expected. It is a cricket stadium after all. I hadn't thought of that. The lap went too fast, I would have loved to absorb in more of the incredible atmosphere. I found some energy somewhere and dug deep to speed up … and almost sprint, or what felt like it, across the finish line

in 11.09.38. The strangest thing was that I didn't feel exhausted. How weird is that? Isn't it crazy how the body can adapt to anything? Even a diet of energy drinks and bananas!

The finish line closes at 12 hours on the clock. Anyone who doesn't make it in within this time is disqualified. It is torture watching the runners arrive into the stadium with one minute left on the clock and the struggle to make it over the line. For me, these runners have had the hardest job of all. They have struggled to make each cutoff along the way, and every second counts for them as they strive for the line. Watching an older man get a cramp at the final bend and seize up and not cross the line will stay with me. As will the couple who fell over the line together with seconds to spare as the lady fell metres from the finish line.

Next year the route changes to the UpRun. I wonder if there are some unexpected downhills on that route? That might be a nice surprise instead of the uphill this year. Might be enough to tempt me back again. I have that 11-hour target in my head – not to mention the back-to-back medals.

See you next year Comrades. It's true what they say, Comrades has a way of dragging you back.*

*I didn't actually go back the following year, I went on a similar adventure to Italy. But reading this now, I'm tempted again.

7

LOOK AFTER YOURSELF

Your Running Body

Most recreational runners don't set an end date on their running 'careers'. We hope and assume we will be running right into old age. Running becomes so much a part of our identity that leaving it behind would mean that friendships, routine and strength would all be lost from our lives. It is important to plan for our running future and take steps to make sure our bodies and our minds will be able for it. Consider it your running pension.

Minding your body now will pay off in years to come. Being injured, burnt out or basically not enjoying running any more are the reasons why we won't keep it going into the years when we might need it most.

Many of the changes you can make to improve your running and mind your body don't involve running at all. Think about warm up, mobility, strength, nutrition, hydration, posture and rest. Most runners know they should be taking the time to spend a few minutes each day on these elements, but hands up who would rather run an extra mile than spend the minutes future-proofing their running body?

Don't Blame Running

We often blame running for aches and pains when on the road, but a lot of our issues stem from what we are doing when we are not running. There are very few of us who have a body perfect for running. We all have some wear and tear from our years gone by. Ask yourself the following questions:

- Do you wear high heels?

- Do you cross your legs?

- Do you sit a lot?

- Do you always carry things on one side?

- Are you stressed?

- Are you tired?

- Do you use a laptop?

- Do you live on your phone?

It's impossible in today's world to avoid most of the conveniences that are out there which in theory make our lives better. With sedentary desk jobs, online shopping, washing machines, cars, vacuum cleaners and comfortable couches we have less need to move than ever before. Add to this Netflix, Facebook and convenience food and it's very easy to avoid moving at all – when we are tired after a day's work it is so tempting to collapse on the couch. No wonder that when we do eventually manage to get ourselves out for a run, we feel stiff and creaky.

Nobody's Perfect

Considering everything we are 'supposed' to be doing to help our running, we would never have time to live, not to mention run. We all have busy lives outside the running world, so let's be practical first and accept that we are not going to be able to change our lifestyles completely to fit in around our running demands. We are much more likely to stick to a few small changes than a big one, so begin by thinking about what little changes you could make. Adding a few minutes into your days of exercises, strength work or even mobility can really help. Could you cut five mintues from your run to do these or even multitask them with something else to fit into your day? Even these small steps could really help with your future running life and long-term fitness.

Work in Progress

As a running coach I'm always reading up on the latest tools and tricks to make running better, so I've ended up dabbling with a lot of different approaches to training. Have I found the perfect one? Not yet, but I'm getting closer.

Many runners are fans of Pilates, yoga and weight training as ways to complement their training. Others with less passion for movement enjoy nothing more than a hot bath with Epsom salts to wash away their running aches and pains. There are runners who focus on fine-tuning their running technique to reduce impact while others swear by a good sports massage. There are foam-rolling gurus, ice-bath lovers and runners who will try whatever is new on the market. We are all looking for that little extra to help us feel like a better runner. For what it's worth, I'm currently working on dynamic mobility exercises and breathing techniques to help protect my running body.

One thing I do know as a running coach is that no matter what great intention a runner has, they generally do less than they intend to when it comes to complementary work. The only exception to this is an injured runner who can be very dedicated to getting back on the road. I have suggested to many runners over the years a simple way to fit in what you know your body needs. If you know you won't or can't make the time for a class, try tagging on a few exercises to the end your run. Cutting five minutes off your run and spending those minutes doing some strength or mobility work would be of more value than the extra distance running for most runners.

Running Technique and Chi Running

'It's not running that's bad for your body, it's how you run that damages the body'. **Danny Dreyer, Chi Running Founder**

I never thought about technique when I started running. I was more concerned about getting to the end of the run in one piece without bursting my lungs to have time to consider anything more than putting one foot in front of the other. I just assumed it was my lack of fitness that made running tough. I never thought that it could have been my running technique that made my breathing so laboured and my legs so heavy.

Roll on a few years, however, and all that changed when I set out to train for my first marathon and was petrified I was going to get injured. A few people told me I shouldn't run long distances as I would end up with bad knees. Off to the library I went (pre-internet days) to read up everything I could on technique. I was drawn to a book called *Chi Running*. It promised effortless running and that sounded like what I was after. I practised what I could from the book and realised that by thinking differently about moving, running could actually feel easier. I attended a Chi Running workshop the following year, kept practising and in 2011 was so convinced by its possibilities that I trained as an instructor. Since then I have coached beginners and marathoners and everyone in between to build the principles of Chi Running into their runs.

How do you run?

Stand on the side line of any running event and notice the different ways people move. Just observing their faces, notice how much tension and grimacing can be seen in certain runners. If their face is that uncomfortable, I wonder how the rest of their body feels. Some runners pound their feet and look tired and uncomfortable even when running at a leisurely pace. Others bend over, looking at the ground, and literally drag themselves along. Then there are the runners who look effortless, light and glide along their route. I know which of those runners I'd rather be.

- **Have you considered what you look like when you are running?**
- **How relaxed are you when you run?**
- **Could your running technique be holding you back?**

Look at any young child run, and you will see how relaxed they are. They let their body fall forward, and their feet just keep up with their forward fall. They look effortless and natural and can run all day. Our lifestyles over our school and adult years have impacted our posture and movement patterns and unfortunately most of us run with tense, tight bodies. Chi Running technique aims to give us back some of that running freedom and teaches us how to use more than just our tired legs for power. Instead of using our lower legs to propel the body forward, we aim to use gravity and the core/skeleton to move us forward. This makes running more comfortable and has less impact on the body. It sounds very confusing in words, so I recommend you work with a Chi Running coach or look at some of the online videos to explain how to practise it in your running.

Where to start

Running technique is not going to improve magically. It needs focus and dedication, but it can be kept very simple to start. Try making a few little changes to begin with:

- Stop looking down.
- Pull yourself up out of your hips and imagine you are taller and slimmer than you are, being suspended like a puppet from a string from the top of your head.
- Relax your arms and legs and notice how you now feel tall, confident and strong. Immediately this change will create more space in your lungs, allowing you to take in more air and relieving your breathing. Not only that, you have started using your core, your spinal muscles and your upper body to take the load off your legs. Try it on your next run and notice how much lighter you can feel and how much less effort it takes to run.

Less of the plodding

It's reasonably easy to focus on our running technique at the start of a run. With fresh legs, a clear head and great intentions, we feel strong, tall and confident when we leave home. As the run progresses, should breathing become laboured or legs start to feel heavy, staying focused on form becomes increasingly difficult. We get distracted and concentrate more on the finish line, speed or maybe even an awaiting dinner rather than adapt movement to make the run feel better.

The second half of a run is when we need all the help we can get to make our running stay efficient. Spot the difference between a marathoner at five kilometres and at twenty-five kilometres. An effortless runner with an efficient stride in the early stages often looks heavy and plodding a few hours later. It's worth looking at your stride length in an effort to improve your run so it looks as good at the end of a run as at the beginning.

The grand plan with the Chi Running Technique is to hit the ground underneath the body and not stride out in front. Rather than overthink this, the easiest way I have found to teach this technique is to ask my students to imagine they are running on a treadmill. You don't need to stride forward, you just need to lift your feel lightly off the ground behind you to let the road disappear behind you.

The length of our stride has a lot to do with how much effort we use on our run. A long stride is often not the best thing for a runner. When we stride out in front of our body, our heel generally hits the ground first. This 'heel-strike' has been linked to many injuries due to the impact of the significant force it sends up the body from the heel through the knees, hips and into the lower back. The rear leg also has to work extra hard to move the body forward to overcome the 'brake effect' of the heel-strike. It's no wonder so many runners are fatigued in the latter kilometres after the lower legs work constantly overtime.

Instead of long strides and leg power, Chi Running focuses on shorter strides and using the rest of the body as well as gravity to help move the runner forward. With a quicker turnover of the legs, we don't have time to stretch our legs forward and heel-strike. Instead we hit the ground closer to our body with a midfoot strike and reduce the impact and the braking effect of the heel strike. When you run with a quicker cadence (shorter stride length), you take more steps, but each of these steps requires less effort and in turn your body stays fresher for longer. The simplest way to experiment with stride length is to let your steps fall into the rhythm of a beat.

Find Your Rhythm

Running to a beat is the single most effective way I have found of keeping my technique fresh and my cadence quick and consistent, especially when I feel my concentration has lapsed. Put simply, it takes the thinking out of technique at the times when my head is overloaded and needs a little break.

The body loves rhythm and will fall into the beat it hears, just like when running to music or falling in with the stride of a running buddy. The optimal running beat is three beats every second and with each beat equating to a step, that's one hundred and eighty steps per minute. Crazy it may sound, but powerful it is. Whenever I feel like I am losing my form, I turn on the beat on my phone/ metronome. It has a magical effect of making me feel taller and lighter at once. If one hundred and eighty beats per minute (BPM) feels too fast, try starting at one hundred and seventy or even one hundred and sixty-five BPM if you are struggling and build gradually.

You don't even need to buy a metronome. There are many free metronome apps which will happily beat at the rhythm you suggest. Although I have been known to listen to the beat for a whole marathon, I understand if you cannot face listening to the beep for a long time. You are not the only one. There has been such an interest in running cadence that the music companies such as Spotify now have options for you to select to play music at the beat that is right for you.

When we tire we are all liable to start to plod. The beat stops us staying too long on the ground and moves us onto the next step without having to concentrate too much. Most of the students I have coached report that their running feels less effort, more relaxed and lighter when running to the beat. With the amount of steps you take in a marathon, or even a 5k, anything that can help your steps feel better is at least worth an experiment. Try it out – as you practise, you will notice that your body position may change and you will lead your run with your body rather than your legs, allowing gravity to kick in, and feeling like you are being pulled along the road.

Like any practice, Chi Running works on the basis of gradual progression. I like to introduce technique gradually, adding in one component at a time for my students. Like any movement or exercise, it's hard to describe in words; you need to practise, have someone video you, see and feel the difference and keep on at it. Don't worry if it takes time to get the hang of it – just enjoy the fact that there are tools we can all upon to make our bodies feel better, lighter and more comfortable when we are having an off day.

Chi Running is not the only running technique out there but it's the one that has carried me around many long-distance events. There are other running techniques for sprinters and long distance, so I encourage you to read up and find what works for you. If you can find a coach locally, do invest in at least one training session as its very hard to know if what you are reading in a book is being applied correctly. Nothing beats the expert eye.

While it is great to learn good technique as a beginner, it's never too late. Many an experienced runner has wondered how they managed to run for so long without ever thinking about how they run. When I teach workshops now I have runners who are brand new to running and want to start right. I also have injured runners who are looking at technique as a last resort. Each of these runners knows their own body better than I ever can, but all of them pick up some tips and tricks they can apply to help them when running feels uncomfortable and heavy.

Aoife and her metronome: dear Garmin, I love you, but ...

For years I have loved running. Correction – I have loved the post-run feeling. I can scarcely remember a time when going for a run was just that. It was always in training for something, to get faster, to go further, to be better than my last run. For a while that worked as I was always improving. Then a few things in my life changed and running could no longer be my number one focus. Also, I needed my runs to be less pressured and more about fun and escapism. The first thing I always did when my watch beeped on a run was check my time, and my pace and my distance, and then when I got home I uploaded my run to Garmin and analysed it. I needed to reduce my dependency on my watch and times and paces.

A good friend (some know her as Mary) had been preaching the benefits of metronome running for some time and I never got around to it. So, one day she handed me one and told me to ignore my watch and just run to the beat. If I'm honest I was sceptical; how would I know how far I had run, how fast I was going and more important if I got a PB? So off I set, initially it was different listening to the constant beep. Then I forgot I was even running. I was so relaxed, all of a sudden thirty minutes had passed and I could have continued for ever (at least in my head I could). From that day I was hooked.

The next challenge was a 10k race with my new partner, the metronome. Everything about the race and the day before was different, I didn't have pre-race nerves, I didn't have the jitters I usually have. I was worried I would get carried away with the crowd but much to my surprise I stuck with my beat and enjoyed the race more than I have ever enjoyed a run before. As the kms ticked by, I was comfortably overtaking people and even coming across people I knew I was able to have a brief chat to them before heading on my way. All of a sudden we hit 5k. How that happened I have no idea, I was still so relaxed. So on I continued, I knew the 2nd half of this route was tougher than the 1st so not celebrating just yet. Still going strong at 6, 7, 8k and my pace was quickening without any effort. How was this possible? This is the magic of relaxed running. I completed the race in a great time and probably would have been slower had I set off at a ridiculous pace with pressure for time and PBs that were unachievable for me.

Thank you, Mary, and thank you to my new bestie, my metronome.

Over the Hill

Running on a hill is a great way to practise both your running technique and your positive head games. When supporting a race, I will always cheer at a point where runners are on an uphill stretch. It's the time when they need most support, where their motivation is at its lowest and where their head is telling them to walk. It's interesting to watch the different runners from this spectator position. I notice how many runners seem to make hills a lot harder on their bodies than they need to. Many associate running uphill with effort, muscle soreness, breathlessness and fatigue. For this reason, they choose to avoid hills in training and struggle on race day or when they do encounter a hill they cannot avoid.

Visualisation can work great on a hill: I like to imagine that I'm running on an escalator so the ground is moving upwards with me and carrying me along with it. Be aware that wherever there is an uphill, there is a downhill close by. The more practice you get, the less intimidating hills will become, and the more positive your mindset will be. Make a choice to decide that hills are good for you, that you are able for them and that you are good at running them. After that, any hill becomes a welcome challenge.

The mechanics of hill running

The majority of runners attempt to run fast up the hill with long strides with a view to getting it over as quickly as possible. Others appear to be in denial and keep their heads down hoping that they will reach the top quicker by not knowing what's ahead. Both of these types arrive at the top breathless with their legs burning. This is no surprise as they have tensed their face and body, reduced their lung capacity and overworked their leg muscles on the way. Alongside these runners are those who slow down to a walk long before they need to. All of these runners never seem to consider that running a little slower might make the hill slightly easier.

If you think Chi Running Technique is useful on the flat, you will really benefit from it on hills. Applying a few simple strategies to making the hill easier helps runners of all levels. If you are bending at the waist and looking down at the ground, you have instantly reduced your lung capacity and started to overuse your legs. Instead:

- Make the uphill a whole-body effort.
- Look where you are going and imagine yourself being taller than you are – the feeling of being tall gives you more space for air.
- Imagine that the person in front of you has a string pulling you along behind them. Keep your eye on their back.

The larger the steps we take, the more we use our calves and leg muscles to power the hill. Small steps are key to taking pressure off your calves and quads. They also prevent you from over-striding and bending at the waist.

- Use the image of the hill being a stairway and run up like you are running upstairs.
- Avoid running on your toes.
- Relax your lower legs.

You will use less effort in your legs, your feet will land much closer to your body and you will need a lot less muscle power to move forward into the next step. We cannot use gravity to help us on an uphill, unfortunately, so it's helpful to call on the extra resources of our back muscles and our arms.

- Driving the arms upwards and forwards at the same beat as your small steps will help lift you up the hill.
- Avoid tensing the shoulders and wrists.
- Keep the shoulders down but imagine you are punching up towards your cheeks.

If you think you cannot run up the hill, you probably won't. Break the hill into small chunks. Distract yourself from getting to the top by focusing only on getting to a particular landmark. Focus on the step you are in and what you are doing in that step to make your body as relaxed and comfortable as possible. Count steps if that helps.

Having said all that, there may well come a time on a hill where walking makes more sense than running. On a very steep uphill, it's very common to overuse the calf muscles by running on toes. This might be the perfect time to walk and conserve energy. Don't feel like a failure for doing this.

Strength for Runners

If you end up at the physiotherapist with a running injury you will most likely get prescribed some form of strength work and be told to take a break from running while you recover. While a strength training session in a gym tailored for your body would be an excellent start, I know many of you are already discounting that as an option. It's not that you don't agree that its good, it's that you just know you won't go. We often associate fitness with gyms and fitness classes taking up at least one hour of our valuable time. If the prospect of one hour of fitness is intimidating or impossible to fit into your schedule, try something a little more manageable from the comfort of your own home.

One Minute a Day

Let's get started simply. I challenge you to one minute of exercise per day. You don't need any equipment, you don't need a gym or fancy Lycra clothing and, most important, you don't even need any base level of fitness. Enough of the excuses, we all have one minute of our day that goes unaccounted.

A favourite exercise is the plank and a great one to see progression over time. From posture to strength, it has huge benefits for us all in just one minute. If you do have any injuries that might restrict you doing this, please choose a different exercise such as walking/ running up and down the bottom step of your stairs for one minute. It's all about finding something that is a challenge for you but also something that is pain-free and achievable.

Let's get started today. If you are liable to forget, set an alarm on your phone for a regular time when you know you will be in a location where you can do your exercise every day. Get a calendar and pop it up on your fridge. Tick off each day that you complete the exercise. Start with the challenge today and then see if you can do a streak of three days or even five days. My aim for you would be to eventually complete a full week of the challenge. If you can do that, you will be much closer to building the habit and reaching a month of successful tick boxes in your calendar. Don't put it off any longer. Go for it and enjoy that smug feeling of knowing you are heading in the right direction of beginning to complement your running.

How to plank

When doing the plank, it is important to build up gradually and slowly. Choose from the two levels in the picture. Do not attempt the more advanced level (on toes) until you are very comfortable at the initial level (on knees). Only when you can do the knees for one minute non-stop should you consider moving to the toes. Be patient. One minute a day will add up but do not expect to be perfect from the start. Pay special attention to your body position and avoid tension in shoulders and back. Remember to breathe too!

Build it Up

As time goes on you will feel more confident and might even consider adding in extra exercises to your mini routine. You will be motivated to improve, and extra minutes and exercises will come. Consider adding lunges, squats, wall sits, side planks or even stretches to parts of your body that you know need it.

You can create your own routine. You might even consider working out your upper body. Most of us are a lot stronger in our legs and lower body than our upper body, and shy away from upper-body work. Don't be scared, I don't suggest you need to be lifting heavy weights and hanging out of bars (although they are skills we surely could work on). Instead, start at the basics and build up to being able to do push ups. Start out with standing push ups against a wall and gradually lower your body position, using walls, benches, chairs and even the steps of a stairs to work the body more as it progresses. There is nothing as motivating as noticing our body changing and being able for more than it was yesterday.

Be aware that this book is not intended to be a training manual to show you the exercises in detail. Pictures, videos and the help of a good coach in person or even online will be better than any words. Instead I would like this piece on strength to point you in the right direction and show you that by taking baby steps we can surely get places. We can all read a book and look at the instructions, but getting down and doing the exercises is the real challenge. You can see videos, tips and advice on all these exercises on ForgetTheGym. ie. Exercise along with the video instead of trying to work out if you are doing it right from a lengthy description in a book.

Plank a day challenge

During the Lent of 2014 our Forget The Gym coach Anne took on the challenge of an exercise every day in Lent. Anne was so happy with her results she decided we should share the idea and our 'plank a day' challenge was born. Since then, we have more than two thousand people taking on the challenge with the support of our daily reminders on Facebook and we have seen some exciting results. From fitness to confidence, the changes have been enormous.

Many of the people who signed up to the challenge live in areas where classes are not available or have commitments that don't allow them the freedom to go to a gym. Some did it alone, others roped in their families and friends. Everyone kept accountable by keeping track of their progress, posting pictures of their planks and reminding and supporting each other along the way. The challenge was originally for one month but years later we still bring it back to get people back into routines that they have let slip.

Motivation has come from the photos and memories we have from those taking part. We have had planks after races, on holidays, in Disneyland, at Base Camp Everest, on the Great Wall of China, poolside, in playgrounds, in parks, by the fire, at the Taj Mahal, at hen parties and down along the Cliffs of Moher.

Some dedicated plank students have kept it going themselves even without our constant nagging. Five students did a plank every day for a year and one extra keen plank master Lorraine was so taken by it that she has completed over 700 days of a plank in a row to date. Her husband has even created an app for her to remind and record the plank progress. You won't get to 700 days, however, if you don't start at one and that is the purpose of the group, to get you started and help you get motivated to create a long-term habit. Could you create your own month or even week-long challenge to get yourself started?

Recovery for Runners

We are a strange breed, us runners. Some of us would rather put ourselves through a few fast intervals than relax. Most of our recovery strategies are nice things to do, yet we tend to cut corners on them. Try your best to build them into your training. Generally the more running you are doing, the more time you need to be spending on recovery. Find out what works best for you and build it into your plan. Everyone is different, but the principle is the same – look after your body and it will perform better for you.

Sleep

It doesn't get any easier than sleeping, yet we are all guilty of letting time in the evening run away from us. Remember that the body repairs itself when we sleep: all of us could benefit from an extra hour or two each night. Keep track of how much you are sleeping for a week and even noting the numbers will make you more aware of where you are losing out. It is often mentioned that the time the body repairs best is between 10 p.m. and 1 a.m. Are you asleep then?

Ice baths

I know this sounds absolutely awful, but I promise it's one of the best things for the legs after a long run. Don't bother putting yourself through the torture if you are running shorter distances, but if you are training for long distance I highly recommend it. You don't necessarily need ice, just the cold water in the bath tends to be cold enough. As soon after your run as you can, hop in. Make it easy on yourself and keep your running clothing on (apart from the runners). Or make yourself a cup of tea. I recommend phoning someone who understands your situation and helping them distract you while you get in. The first minute is pretty challenging but you will be surprised that it gets easier. Say in for ten minutes if you can. When you get out you will have new legs! The cold makes your legs feel so light after the run. Even better, if you can put your legs in the sea after the run, you will get the benefit of the salt water too and will be able to wade in gradually rather than take the big dip.

Hot baths

Always follow the cold bath with a hot shower or bath. This is where you can treat yourself. Include some bath salts, Epsom salts, seaweed, whatever you fancy, and enjoy a little time to yourself.

Put your feet up

Leg drains are one of the nicest ways to make your legs feel lighter and fresher with very little effort. Position yourself close to a wall (or tree), stick your feet up at a right angle to your body, and relax. Stay for at least ten minutes. The fresh blood will flow into your legs when you come back up to standing (do this gradually) and you will feel fresher and more comfortable. Try this after a long run, or any time when your legs are tired.

Switch off

We all have different ways to switch off. Although running can be our 'mindful' time, switching off from it can be good too. Sometimes, the right thing to do is forget about all things running-related. Go to the cinema, visit a friend (who has no interest in running), read a book (that's not about running). The change of focus is good, especially if you are training for a big event or you are finding that you are getting anxious about running.

Sports massage

Getting to know a good sports therapist/physiotherapist is a great thing – someone who knows your body and can advise what you need to work on can help you avoid injury and pay the right attention to your body. Many runners would be lost without their regular 'rub' which helps loosen out tight spots. When training for long distance, I recommend one sports massage per month as the mileage gets longer. A good therapist will be able to notice how the long distance is impacting your body and what you should be doing to help it. By the way, any notions you have of relaxing spa-like massages will quickly disappear once you are on the massage table. A sports massage is not exactly relaxing; let's just call it energising instead.

Foam rolling and massage balls

Foam rollers have become a new tool for sports people in recent years. Some use them for warm up, others for strength training, but most runners I know use them as an opportunity to roll out the kinks in their body. Consider this more of a self-inflicted type of massage. Working out how to get your body into the right position to roll can be like a game of Twister but once you know what you are doing, it can become a lovely regular 'training session' which can easily take place while watching TV, being on a phone call or supervising a Lego-building session.

While the thought of the foam roller doesn't always appeal to me, I am a huge fan and a very regular user of a massage ball, or should I say any reasonably hard ball somewhere between the size of a golf ball and tennis ball. I have them dotted around the place and will pick them up and use to roll out tight glutes or most likely roll my feet. If you have never done it, give it a go. It's as simple as it sounds. Roll your feet over the ball, putting as much pressure as feels right and you will notice a few minutes later how much lighter your feet feel. Consider how much our feet have to put up with being trapped in running shoes, and other shoes, all the time. They deserve a chance to have a little massage too.

Food and Drink

There are endless books on the shelves on healthy eating and improving performance for runners. Fear not, I'm not going to force you down any restrictive diet or apply any complicated mathematics on percentages of carbs and protein in your meals. You know your body better than anyone. A bad diet won't directly make you injured but it will impact your energy, focus and recovery.

We are all aware of what makes us feel good and what makes us feel stodgy and heavy. There are times when we eat well and others when we don't. Rather than tell you what to eat, I believe if you just apply a little bit of planning to your food you can eat better for your running without becoming a food bore. Observe the impact of your food choices on running and recovery: we want our food to nourish us; give confidence in our running ability, clarity in our mind and energy in our legs. I also recognise that we don't have all day to spend cooking.

I love my food and I have more cookery books than running books. Yet I don't see the point in becoming obsessed with restricting foods. That surely is shortcut to being miserable and feeling guilty when you do break out. Instead, if we are 'generally' good most of the time, the cake and coffee after a run is more part of the experience than something to feel guilty about.

When I coach runners, I never mention weight. I don't promise any quick fixes or inch losses. Weight loss is not the goal. The goal is to get out the door and enjoy running. While indeed the two may well go hand in hand for many runners, I would hate our running success to be determined only by how much weight we have lost. Surely how we feel in ourselves is a better measure?

Healthy choices are easy to make when the food is in front of you, but when we are tired and rushed it's harder to do. If you don't have the correct food available, you will end up eating something that is ready-made and processed, therefore less nutritious. Think ahead.

My mother always made the point that if there was a bowl of cut fruit in the fridge it would be eaten, but a fruit bowl on the table could go untouched for days. If you don't have a mammy in the house preparing your nice food for you, it's time to take responsibility yourself. What you eat on your running days doesn't need to be complicated, but it does need to be planned. The time of the day we prefer to run can determine our food choices and volume.

Morning runners

Many morning runners will run on an empty stomach rather than get up extra early to let food digest and move through their system before they run. The most important thing is to find food that agrees with your stomach. It is an experiment but why not try out some pre-run breakfast options that my runners have found useful for their running bodies?

- Nothing – if you can't face getting up early enough
- A glass of orange juice (if you can't stomach food)
- Homemade granola, yoghurt and fruit
- Porridge
- Toast and banana

If you have the luxury of time after your morning run, enjoy a leisurely breakfast. If not, get organised the night before and have it ready to go, so you don't rush out the door without giving your body the fuel it needs to recover from the run and replenish energy for the day. The same food choices for breakfast before the run work for afterwards. If it happens to be a weekend and the morning is your own, take advantage. Eggs are a popular post-run brunch/breakfast, whether they are disguised in fruity pancakes or piled high scrambled on sourdough. There is something about a post-run weekend brunch that makes the day feel like a holiday. Up, run and brunch. What endorphins to have in the system to fuel the day!

Evening runners

The evening runner will benefit most from a healthy breakfast and a wholesome lunch with a mid-afternoon snack to keep energy up until the evening run.

Here are some mid-afternoon snack options:
- Fruit
- Yoghurt
- Nuts
- Hummus with crudités for dipping
- Popcorn
- Crackers with cheese

Many an evening runner won't feel particularly hungry after the run, so having dinner at lunchtime can mean that a light post-run meal will see them through the rest of the evening.

My post-run light evening meals include:
- Pitta bread with spinach, chicken, pesto and tomatoes
- Cheese omelette and brown bread
- Avocado on toast
- Cheese/crackers and fruit
- Roasted chickpeas and vegetables

Other evening runners return home ravenous. If you're in this camp, be sure to have the food prepared before your run, or appoint someone at home to be the chef so you can shower and eat before the evening disappears and you have time to digest before bed.

Lunchtime runners

If you are organised enough to run on your lunch break, it is a wonderful way to break up the day. Make sure you eat well at breakfast time and maybe have a light snack around 11 a.m. Whatever you plan on eating for lunch, have it ready to go for when you return. Don't ruin a run by having to rush to the shop to buy lunch and then inhale it in a few minutes. You might even feel like eating gradually over the afternoon rather than immediately. If you have been limiting your fluids in the morning knowing you were planning a run, hydrate well again in the afternoon. A great post-run lunch would include both protein and carbohydrates, so that pretty much leaves you open to choose whatever you fancy.

Fuelling for Long Distance

Have you ever tried eating and running at the same time? It is a skill and an experiment for sure. From the biscuit that crumbles and dries out your mouth to the jelly sweet that sticks your teeth together, long-distance runners have the added concern of finding the right fuel that not only can they swallow but that also agrees with their stomach.

Any run up to ten kilometres should not require you to eat any food on the run. Your body should have enough in its system to keep you going. Food for long-distance running can be very complicated but it doesn't need to be. Keep it simple by following these six easy tips.

1 Hydrate midweek

Keeping hydrated is a full-time job, not something you should think about thirty minutes before your run. Our bodies are made up of 70 per cent water; our brains are 90 per cent water. A slight decrease in this balance has an impact on running performance, co-ordination, balance, concentration, reaction time and general wellbeing. For a runner this links to fatigue, muscle cramps and potential injury. Keep hydrated every day and you won't need to do anything different on long run days; just maybe don't drink too close to running.

2 Work out your pre-race dinner

The food you eat the night before will fuel you for your run. Eat foods that you normally eat and that you know agree with your system. Avoid trying anything new or heavily spiced. There is no perfect pre-race dinner – just choose what makes you feel confident the following morning. For years spaghetti Bolognese was my go-to pre-marathon meal, easy to make at home and available practically everywhere if I was eating out. Choose something that makes you sleep easy, digests well and is ideally not still jumping around in your stomach the next morning when you start running.

3 Time your perfect breakfast

Breakfast choices and timing are a very individual digestive decision. Practise what breakfast works for you and how long you need to leave before running. It may be eggs, toast, cereal, a banana, porridge or something else. If you are feeling hungry during a long run it's a sign you need to have more in your system, so try larger portions in your meals in the days before the run.

4 Eat on the run

Your training runs are the best times to experiment with foods and drinks that will sit well in your tummy. There is an array of choices and you can be as natural or artificial in your fuelling choices. Check out Chapter 9 on long-distance running to find out more.

5 Cool down with a snack

It is often suggested that we should eat a little carbohydrate and protein within thirty minutes of finishing a long run. Most runners I know cannot stomach anything too substantial after running so having a light snack in the car, or a drink, tends to be all they will be able for.

6 Repair your body

Aim to eat a good meal within two hours of finishing a training session. What we may crave after a run may not be what our body needs, so a little planning on these post-run meals makes all the difference. While we may feel we deserve to indulge after our long run, remember that what we eat in the twenty-four hours after our run is what the body will use to repair and replenish itself. What we eat and drink before a run can impact more than our energy. Many a runner has had to deal with a toilet issue on the run.

Where's the Toilet?

The need to pee

From peeing to even light leaking, there are a lot of people who struggle to manage this issue with running. Trying to avoid the need to go is an art in itself. The more you think about it, the more you need to go and often it can feel quite random when it occurs. Be conservative with your fluids on a running day, and avoid caffeine as it's a diuretic and will only exacerbate the issue.

There are many runners (and non-runners) who have issues with pelvic floor muscles and leaking. Unfortunately, it's one reason many runners (particularly women) give up on running. Running motion can indeed magnify the issue. Post-baby the problem can increase and while runners may be prescribed exercises to do, new mums are often too busy to do them so the running gets put on the long finger. It's an issue close to my heart as I struggled with this problem post-baby and it has sent me down a long road of research into its source. In fact, the cause has been linked not to skipping exercises but the opposite. Many of us have pelvic floor muscles that are too tight from overworking and we need to focus on relaxing the muscles rather than tightening them even more. I have learnt so much more about my body as I research this topic and continue to delve into this research which for the main part is unspoken in running circles. If you think it's a concern for you, a women's health physiotherapist is a great place to start. Apart from the joy of an internal examination, you will be advised on the best direction you need to go to help your body.

Runners' trots

Whatever about having the need to pee, feeling a sudden need to poo is actually something many runners have experienced, some regularly; others only very occasionally. When running, our insides jiggle up and down and get mixed about so much that it's no wonder so many runners' intestines are affected. Thankfully I'm not one of them, but I've been asked many times by runners, particularly long-distance ones, for tips to help ease this urge.

- First, I think that most runners spend more time worrying about needing to go to the loo than actually needing a mid-run pitstop. If you know the location of every toilet en route, even if it is in a pub or petrol station, it gives you the confidence of knowing there is always a 'comfort stop' in easy reach.
- Our food choices and timing can help our bodies with the issue. Personally, if I have caffeine before a run, or have a gel/sweet that includes caffeine when on a run, my stomach doesn't thank me. While some runners enjoy caffeine for the kick it gives them, we need to be aware of its impact on our stomach too as it is a diuretic.
- Artificial sweeteners such a sorbitol have been linked with urgent toilet need as well as high fibre and dairy.
- To give extra security, in every sense, carrying a little plastic bag and a few wipes might make you more relaxed if you do need to hide behind a bush!

Having said all that, it really is an individual situation so please try your own experiments. I believe the best way to learn how your body works is to time how long food takes to go through your system and work your running around that. Ideally if you can 'go' before you start running that makes a run a lot more comfortable. While I do know runners who take a tablet to prevent diarrhoea, I would almost never recommend that. Instead practise, experiment and do what you can to reduce your anxiety.

Mobility for Runners

I have spent a lot of time researching mobility, which has become a buzzword in running and other sporting circles. I'm constantly noticing which parts of my body are moving well and which are not. Regardless of how flexible our muscles are from stretching, our range of motion in our joints and our ability to move freely helps us move better and efficiently, whether it is in running or in life. Many of the mobility exercises and tips can be built into our life rather than set aside as exercise time.

There are simple, fun and practical things we can all do to move more and move differently and as the years go on we need to work at our mobility harder if we fancy being sprightly, active pensioners.

Should I Stretch?

Some runners consider a run incomplete without stretching; others consider stretching a waste of time. There is endless research and constantly changing theories on what stretching we should or should not be doing as runners. I believe that if you feel better after stretching then you should do it.

I know that I overuse my neck and shoulder muscles. For this, I blame years of laptops and cars and I have to constantly remind myself when I'm running to relax my shoulders. I certainly benefit from neck stretches so I build them into my day. When my neck and shoulders are looser the rest of my body relaxes more too. A lot of runners feel the same way about their calves: if they loosen out tight calves they feel relief not just in their calves but up their legs and into their lower back.

By stretching we notice where we might be tight or where one side of the body feels more restricted then the other. Many runners love yoga for this purpose. Although there are many more benefits to yoga than just flexibility, the opportunity to spend dedicated time in lengthening positions is very beneficial for runners.

Don't stretch if you feel it doesn't work for you, but if you are constantly feeling tight somewhere, don't blame your running, blame your lack of time balancing out running. Set a timer for ten minutes and just stretch and move in whatever way feels good. Follow an online yoga video, or better still find a local class. It's very easy to be distracted at home – you won't wander off to make a cup of tea or check your Facebook if you are in a yoga studio.

I could give you detailed instructions of how to do lots of stretches but pictures speak louder than words. Here are some ideas of stretches you could try. Experiment with them and find the few you benefit from most, then find a way to build them into your day.

Don't stretch to the point that you feel pain. The stretch should feel lengthening and comfortable. Stretching beyond this will only cause the muscles to tighten even more.

Most experts agree that holding stretches should not be done just before running. It's better to stretch a body that is warm. A more mobile warm up such as walking and dynamic (moving) stretching is considered better as you are not stretching a cold muscle and hence the injury risk is reduced. Keep the body moving in a warm up, then at the end of the run consider holding the stretches for longer as part of your cool down.

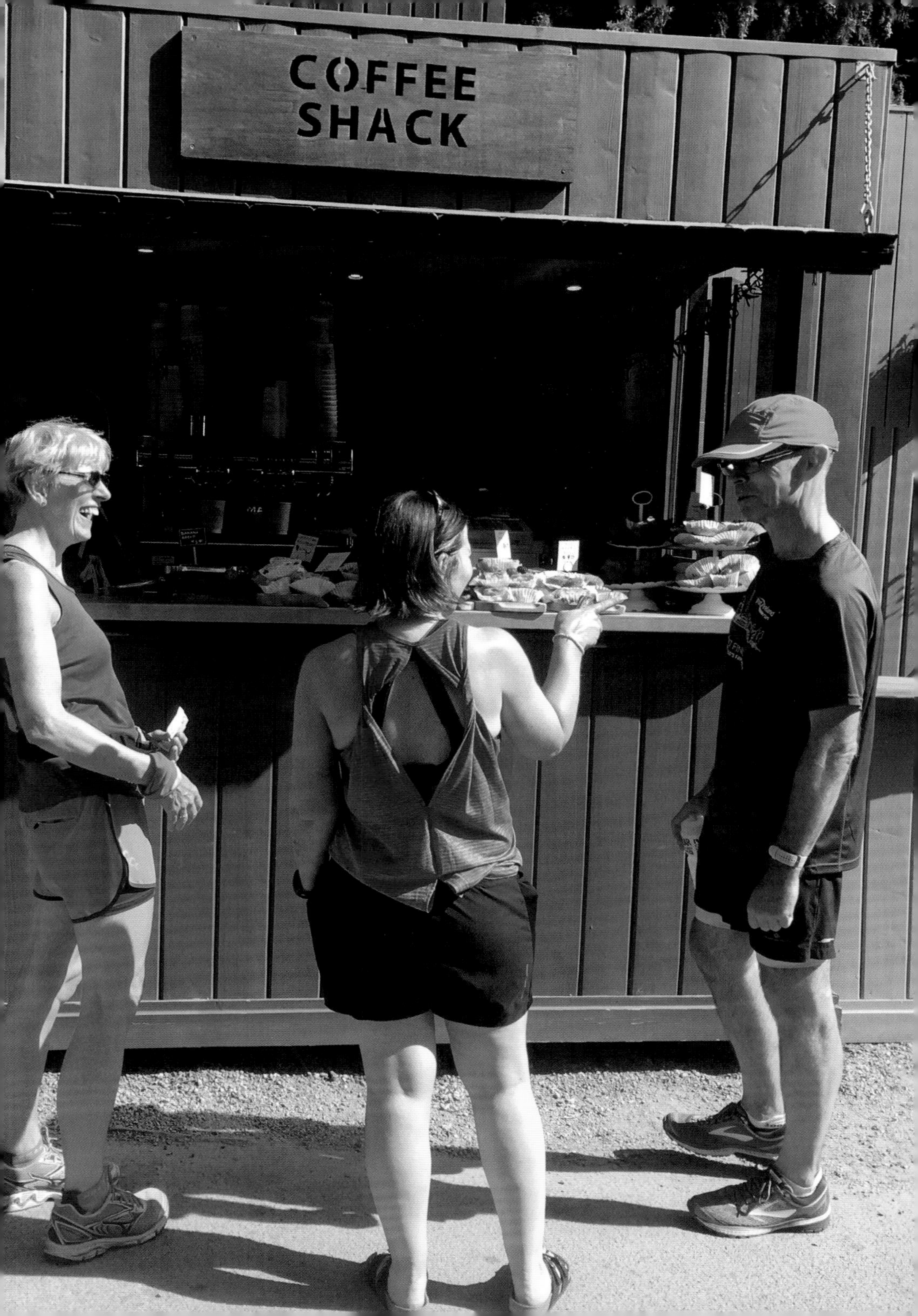
COFFEE
SHACK

8

PREPARE
FOR RACE DAY

Train Your Head

Have the following thoughts ever popped into your mind when running a race?

- Why am I doing this?
- I'm not going to be able to hold this speed – I feel wrecked.
- Everyone else looks so comfortable – I feel like I'm fading.
- Is that a pain in my knee? Maybe it's an injury.
- Should I stop, walk for a few minutes and get my breath back?
- Maybe I haven't trained enough, I should have done more.
- Here comes a hill, I won't be able to run up it.
- Everyone is overtaking me – I'm not able for this.
- I hate running, I'm never signing up for anything else again!

Sound familiar? Notice what you are telling yourself when you are running. If you are filling your head with negative thoughts this will transfer to your running. As your confidence drops, you will start to lose your posture, good technique and you will become heavier on your feet.

On other days you might have positive thoughts going through your head which completely change your approach to the race.

- I feel strong – there are no aches or pains.
- This is easier than I thought it would be.
- I'm overtaking people – they don't seem as strong as me.
- I feel tall, confident and relaxed.
- I love running, this feels great.
- I think I can go faster – I'm going to make the end.
- The pace feels comfortable, the training is paying off.

Everything is easy when you have this positive mindset. The challenge is how to turn a run where we have a negative mindset into a positive one. While we could focus on technique and muscle relaxation, the added big piece in the jigsaw is the head. It is all about knowing what to say to your doubting mind that will help it rise up and get over the slump.

Sports Psychology for Runners

Sports psychology teaches us how to stay calm and positive, avoid anxiety, deal with doubts and achieve our best performance on race day by training our head as well as our legs. You may think it is just for elite athletes, but in fact, it is just as valuable for recreational athletes as nerves and doubts can hit anyone, whether it's your first 5k or your attempt to win a marathon.

Sport psychology techniques and exercises take practice and will only work on race day if you start integrating them into your training and working out what fits best for you. While useful for all distances, I believe the longer you are running, the more time you have to question your ability and the more you need a positive voice to keep your head strong as your body tires.

I have never been as well prepared for anything in my entire life. Anything. I've done very important things – like big job interviews and giving birth to babies – without the same level of preparation that went into last weekend. You have taught me a big lesson about the value of preparation and what can be achieved when you prepare properly. Believing you can do something, really truly believing it, is more than half the battle. You enabled me to believe in myself in a way that no one ever has and in a way that would not have been possible for me to achieve without your magical blend of warmth and professionalism. Last weekend I ran the Dublin Marathon, I got no blisters, I did not chafe, I still have all my toenails and I ENJOYED EVERY STEP. Thank you, Mary.
Niamh

Pre-Race Nerves

Much of race day anxiety comes down to runners not being organised and getting overwhelmed by logistics. We may not have the luxury of a support team to help with preparations for our race day, so we need to be even more organised when it comes to knowing what to bring, where to go and what to wear.

As race day approaches you should know your pre-race breakfast, race day clothing, food, drinks, gadgets and everything else that is important for you for race day such as the route, the hilly sections and the toilet locations.

There are certain things we cannot prepare for that may happen on race day. We can, however, plan what we will do if they do happen. Make a list of all the things you are worried about and then write the solution – what you will do if they do happen. This will avoid much of the anxiety and panic of worrying about the onset of a dodgy stomach, a family emergency, bad weather or an alarm clock not going off. Control what you can control but accept that there are certain things that you cannot take responsibility for. Just having this list on paper takes the worry out of your head and you can add to this list as worries appear and disappear throughout your training period.

Being nervous and anxious uses up valuable energy. Save your energy for your run and instead trust in your training, work on developing your belief and confidence, and bring back your positive mindset by focusing on what is in your control. There will be times when you feel overwhelmed both in training and on race day. Accepting that there will be bad training days and bad kilometres along each run is the starting point. Knowing what to do to manage them is the key. Learning techniques to keep calm, relax the body and save energy can help all runners. These skills need to be practised and won't magically work if you don't apply them regularly in training.

Countdown to Race Day

The best way to arrive at a race start line is nice and early, confident that all the preparation is done and grateful that you are in a position to take on the event. However, it's a lot more likely you might be rushing, anxious and possibly doubting your ability. The key elements that go into making a race day a success are everything we have discussed already. Having dedicated the time to preparation, you can really appreciate and enjoy the event itself. Although, however well preparation has gone, it is normal to have a few butterflies in the stomach. Even the best athletes experience this.

When I train runners for a race, I want them to finish happy, proud, injury-free and possibly looking forward to the next challenge. By the time they reach the week of the race, their training is practically done and all that remains for me to do is to remind them of the things they can do to make the day the best it can be. In the few days leading up to the event it's time to rest the legs, train the head and prepare the bags and maybe even some supporters. The race itself is, in fact, the reward for the training. When you have prepared well, you can enjoy the event, be grateful you can get out there and run, and in many cases surprise yourself with your capabilities.

No amount of extra mileage on race week is going to improve your performance on race day. Less is more and it's better to wind down the distances and instead make the time to get your head in the right place for race day. Don't waste your energy pondering on what could happen; instead focus on practical things you can do to avoid anxiety and set yourself up for a great day out.

- Research all you can about the route and the race day logistics.
- Drive the route in your car or watch the route map video.
- Identify where water stations and toilets are located along the route.
- Get an idea of any hilly terrain and avoid any surprises.
- If you get an opportunity, run the last kilometre of the race route. Being familiar with the finish will allow you imagine yourself being there and plan for what lies ahead.
- Avoiding uncertainty is one of the best ways to reduce pre-race anxiety and help keep calm.

You will not get any fitter during race week, but you can get stronger and better prepared by making time to allow your body rest, repair and get ready for the main event. Not many of us sleep well the night before the big day, so take the pressure off and bank your sleep early in the week so you are less anxious about getting good rest the night before race day. Similarly, consider your food and hydration. Start early in the week by preparing good food, shopping for weekend essentials and keeping well hydrated. These are simple tasks but are often forgotten.

Try not to tell everyone you are running or share too much information about your race until it is done. Knowing that a social media following is tracking your every move can be great if all is going to plan but not quite so much fun if things don't work out the way you'd hoped. By all means post your medal, your smile and your fabulousness afterwards.

Are You All Packed?

Make a list of everything you need to bring you with you on race day. Set out everything you need the night before, so you don't spend the race morning in a fluster trying to find your lucky socks. Wear whatever clothes you would normally wear when running – don't try anything new on the day. If the weather is cool, bring an old jumper that you can wear and throw away at the start line. Also, if it is raining, bring a large black sack which you can wear over your body to avoid getting soaked.

So here is what is on my list:

What to wear	☐ T-shirt ☐ Sports bra ☐ Shorts/leggings ☐ Throwaway jumper ☐ Throwaway gloves ☐ Throwaway hat	☐ Socks ☐ Underwear ☐ Runners ☐ Race number (fill in details on back) ☐ Safety pins ☐ Hair clips/bobbins
Just in case	☐ Vaseline ☐ Plasters/tape ☐ Sunglasses ☐ Tissues ☐ Money (€20 emergency)	☐ Black sack for rain ☐ Contacts' phone numbers ☐ Ziploc bag if wet – for iPod and money
Motivation	☐ Phone (charged) ☐ Watch (charged) ☐ Running belt	☐ Training log/notes/ strategy – to keep you calm ☐ Metronome
Nutrition	☐ Gels/drinks ☐ Sweets	☐ Breakfast food ☐ Jelly Babies
Bag for after	☐ Full change of clothes ☐ Tracksuit/fleece ☐ Change of underwear	☐ Plasters ☐ Loose-fitting shoes ☐ Snacks ☐ Bottled water

Know Your Pace

There is a powerful atmosphere on a race day which pulls you faster than you should go at the start. With fresh legs and buckets of enthusiasm, it takes discipline to hold yourself back. Take a little time to work out your pacing strategy. Decide what your starting pace for the first kilometre/mile should be and don't be tempted to go faster no matter how good you feel at the start. It's much better to reserve that energy for the second half. The biggest mistake runners make is starting too fast. It's better to be overtaking people towards the end than watching everyone running past you. If you start towards the back of the group, you are more likely to pace yourself from the start.

Take the time to warm up before you start running. The shorter the race, the longer your warm up should be. For a 5k or 10k, runners should feel fresh-legged from the start and be focused on their planned pace rather than wasting these first minutes loosening out the creaky joints. For a half marathon or longer, less of a warm up is required as the running pace is slower and managing pace at the start is often a good thing.

Try not to concern yourself with the other runners. There will be people warming up, doing fancy stretches, eating unusual food and looking particularly confident. That's okay. They are probably just as nervous as you are, and there will always be people who are faster, stronger or more athletic-looking than you. Don't compare yourself to them or be intimidated by any conversations you hear at the start line. You are running your own race. Your target is to reach your goal – not their goal. You most likely won't see them again and when you get to the finish line they won't concern you in the slightest, even if you are the final finisher. (Have I just got you panicked that you might be last? Don't be silly, someone has to be last. It most likely won't be you and it's certainly not a concern you should have. Someone finishes last in every event. They still finish.)

In years to come, it's not just the finishing time on the clock you will remember. It's the memories of the race day emotions and your training runs that will stay with you. It's up to you to make those memories ones you will want to revisit. You have an opportunity to make your event a race day to remember.

Imagine Your Future

Visualisation is a technique that takes practice but is hugely helpful as you approach race day and need to stay calm yet confident. I ask my students to do it every day and they find it one of the best things they can do to help their training. It does work, but it won't if you don't practise it regularly.

The visualisation technique involves picturing yourself in a future situation. For us, race day is the one to envisage. Create a short video in your head where you see yourself getting up on race morning, eating breakfast, crossing the start line, pacing your run, fuelling as you had planned and crossing the finish line with a smile. As you get closer to race day this video clip (which will only last a couple of minutes) should become clearer as you can visualise more clearly the route, the terrain, your clothing and the locations of your supporters. Over time it will become so vivid that you will feel it is well within your grasp. Replay the video in your head each day and it will help with positivity and belief.

While you're at it, try to picture your ideal running form: running strong, tall and relaxed. If you can play that image in your head you might be surprised at how your body adapts to feeling that very way. Try calling upon that visualisation when you feel heavy-legged when running.

Trust the Training

You have to have faith in your training approach and all the preparation you have done. Reviewing your training diary and recognising how far you have come helps you believe that your original goals are still possible and, most important, realistic. If you don't believe you can do it before you even start, you won't get any more confident as you progress through race day.

Some runners stick Post-it notes on walls, others use vision boards and some even have tattoos to remind them to remain positive and focused. Get inspired and take a little time to create some positive one-liners that you believe and will inspire you to keep on running. You can write your running mantra on the back of your hand if it helps keep you positive on the run. Simple mantras like 'one mile at a time' or 'I can do it' have provided great focus for runners who get distracted by negativity along the route.

The hand in the picture belongs to Niamh, who trained with me for her first marathon a few years ago. On marathon morning it was wonderful to see how she had taken my advice but made it her own. I had never seen anyone so creatively and visually put their motivation literally at their fingertips. To this day I don't know the meaning of the colours, images or words that were on her hand, but I do know each element meant something special, inspiring and uplifting to her. Whenever she needed a reminder of why she was running a marathon, all she had to do was look at her hand. Since then I have seen many motivating hands that were inspired by this picture of what one woman did to keep her head in the right place on race day.

The Art of Distraction

What should we think about when we are in a race? The more you are working on speed and aiming to hit a particular time target, the more you have to focus on technique, pace, form, and relaxation. We can attempt to focus on our current kilometre to make running easier on the body and mind. Break up the run into manageable chunks and give each of these a particular intention. You may choose to concentrate on an element of technique, breathing, fuelling or even a mindful distraction like counting the number of runners you see wearing green T-shirts for each section. Tick off each milestone as it passes by but don't look too far ahead.

Even with the best of intentions our minds wander. We end up far from thoughts of technique and more likely end up doing some of the following:

- Chatting to other runners.
- Listening to music/audio books.
- Scanning the side lines for familiar faces.
- Admiring the scenery.
- Daydreaming.
- Checking out running gear on other runners.
- Looking at your phone/watch.
- Planning what's for dinner.

Is this a bad thing? Not necessarily. It is only natural that the mind will wander. Most of us cannot sit on a cushion and meditate for a few minutes without other thoughts popping into our heads. Running is no different. If the race goal is to avoid anxiety and stress during the run, and if distracting you at some points from the moment helps, then why not? You take in the environment around you, you engage with others, and minutes can fly by. That said, focusing on your running technique and what you can control will help your performance significantly (see more on mindful running on page 118).

I recommend that despite your distractions you check in on a regular basis with your running form, your breathing and your general condition. Every time I hear a phone beep or see a mile marker in a race I move the attention from my wandering mind back to my body. Those triggers remind me to notice how I am feeling. When we focus on what the body is doing we notice where we are holding tension or feeling uncomfortable. Having a few tricks up your sleeve on how to allow the body to relax, run lighter and with less effort is a great asset. This is where running technique comes into play (See Chi Running, page 137).

The Jelly Baby Warriors

We all have little tricks to give us confidence and strength on the run. One which I have used for many years with my long-distance students is the story of the Jelly Baby warriors. Here is how it works. If you are feeling tired or lacking in drive/focus on your run, pop a Jelly Baby in your mouth. As you chew him, he multiplies into thousands of mini jelly warriors that travel around your body to the points that need a bit of a kick. It takes about ten minutes for them to do their work but pay attention and you will notice how you feel better when the little guys have done their work. Don't believe me? Give it a shot. The mind is a powerful tool and if you believe it you can create it. It has carried many a runner out of a negative spot and right into a positive new kilometre. I just wish I could remember who shared this novel approach with me so I could give them credit. It's simple but so effective.

Go With the Flow

Not all runs work out the way we might expect them to. There are some things that are outside our control and the weather is one of them. We can make our running easier by dressing appropriately, giving our body time to adapt to a particular environment and accepting that the conditions may disappointingly mean that we have to change our race goals due to heat, cold, wind or rain. Many years ago, I learnt this lesson the hard way. Arriving into Lanzarote the night before the marathon may have meant the best flight prices, but arriving into that heat directly from an Irish January was a shock for my body. I spent many kilometres chasing the shade and wishing away the time. Even a few days of acclimatising and hydration would have helped my cause.

Running in all weathers and conditions

Being sensible about when and where we run is important. Most of us fade as soon as we try to run in the heat. Our pace struggles as the body works overtime to keep us cool as our internal temperate rises.

Running in the cold is sometimes a pleasure once we convince ourselves to leave the warmth inside. Nicely cosy at the start, we can find that our body warms up very quickly, however, and can overheat with the extra layers we felt were necessary to leave the house.

Running in the rain can be liberating or miserable depending on your attitude and the distance you have to run. A rainy parkrun will make you feel smug all day, but a marathon through puddles may leave you cold, blistered and disappointed.

Slippery leaves or icy paths mean we run differently as we have to pay more attention underfoot. Running in the dark poses similar challenges and running in a busy area can be challenging, especially if you keep having to dodge people with their heads buried in their phones.

It's easy to get frustrated in all these situations but keeping a realistic perspective on running and training and will make you a more balanced, calmer runner. We are not Olympic runners who have to peak on one given day every four years. We have the luxury of finding another race in the future and have no one to answer to but ourselves. And if you're ever complaining about running, remember that lots of people would give anything to be in your running shoes; make the most of the fact you can be out there and go for it.

Appreciate the Spectators

Where would we be without the spectators and supporters on the side lines? They distract us from the distance. They encourage us to keep moving. They are in awe of the runners and we feed off their energy. A cheer, a smile or word of advice from a stranger can literally bring us runners to tears. Supporters make us feel like we are winning when the winners have long since finished and are back home on the sofa eating pasta. If supporters knew how much we appreciate them, they would be very surprised.

If you have friends or family supporting you, put yourself in their shoes and remember that if it's a long-distance event they too have a long-distance wait so they need to know what to expect and what you expect from them. Give them very limited logistical spectator guidelines, for example:

- Stick to the side of the road you will be running on.
- Stand away from other supporters so they are easier to spot.
- Don't stand on a bend as you will be too focused on not tripping up going around the corner to look up and see them.
- Halfway up a hill is an ideal spot as you can see them well in advance and it will stop you being tempted to walk up the hill!
- If your supporters are bringing children, ask them to pick a viewing point near a toilet, a shop and somewhere with shelter. The last thing you want to be greeted with at the end of your run is a group of wet, cranky, hungry and bored supporters. Kids can really feel a part of the event and some might like to make posters, bring along sweets to offer to runners or even carry a balloon so you see them. That said, I wouldn't be too optimistic that they will remain attentive for very long or that all the sweets will end up in the runners' tummies!

If you do want to feed off the support in a race, you can do one very simple thing: take off your headphones. No one will cheer a runner wearing headphones as they assume you are not listening. When you need the extra help from the crowd, run by the side line, make eye contact with the supporter, smile and no doubt you will receive an encouraging word to guide you as far as the next cheering face.

Run for Charity

Many runners take part in events to support a charity. While this can place a burden on you to raise funds and perform well on the day, it can also be an incredible motivating factor. Having a passion for the charity you are running for has spurred you on to take on the training and the event ahead. You most likely will wear with pride a T-shirt highlighting your cause and the reason you have made such efforts to take on this challenge. Well done – charity runners are inspirations to us all. It is becoming harder and harder to raise funds and people are taking on more extreme challenges in order to stand out from the crowd. Be sensible about the challenge you choose – make it realistic but not too easy. Never forget how many people you might encourage by your actions. Run tall, run strong and keep your focus on your reason for being there. Maeve Buckley-Lynch was one such person who was inspired by the charity runners at Dublin Marathon. Her words below capture the atmosphere and emotion of a day that was so special to many.

'GO MARGARET!'

Last year on the marathon bank holiday my house on Crumlin Road was full of cartoons, the smell of toast and the loud sound of small hands sifting through trays full of Lego. Hovering in the air above all this was a sense of anticipation. I stood in the middle of the road outside our house and could see all the way down to the Coombe and beyond. It felt wild to stand on one of the main veins into the heart of Dublin City. Usually it's impossible as it throbs and rumbles, whooshes and squeals. By 9 a.m. there were Gardaí at the corner directing people to access points.

The wheelchair entries flew by first with their incredible strength and then the winners, gazelle-like runners from East Africa. But there was nothing like what was to come. When it happened there were hundreds. Then there were thousands. I left my house and stood on the path outside with my three excited children. There they were, thousands of feet, all falling at different times. At times there was no other sound, just feet, so many of them. The foot rhythm with their breathing was like percussion. It was musical, meditative, spiritual almost.

A lot of these people were out running trying to beat their personal best or reach their target time but so, so many of them were running for another person, someone less able. I gazed at all these incredible people who were using their feet, because they can. Their T-shirt was telling their story, their reason for pounding the hard ground, for putting themselves through such a trial as they were busy taking deep breaths into their diaphragm, concentrating, focusing. On every T-shirt was a different cause. It went on and on, there were so many causes, there were so many bloody diseases. I was moved to tears. I wanted to cry out loud, but my kids might think that I'm totally mad crying at a pack of people running down our road. But my soul is so moved I feel I want to be part of it.

So that is when the tambourines came out, the buckets from the beach were turned upside down and banged upon. Toy drums joined in. At one point myself and my three children were a band! We banged and shook and banged and shook. People clapped and we banged louder. My banging was really trying to say, 'I love you, we are humans, we are all struggling in this bloody mess of disease and love. We are so fragile and we must be strong. We must do this together for each other. The able must help the less able. We are all different but we are all the same.' The world never felt so ridiculously cruel and so wonderfully kind at the same time.

Then I thought that they might be hungry, so the drums went down and the kitchen was raided. What do long-distance runners eat? I had no idea. Fruit? That sounded wise, so every piece was cut up into little bowls. Myself and my children stood at the side of Crumlin Road holding out bowls of apples and mandarins to sweaty strangers. They were so grateful. The children kept shouting 'apples!' 'oranges!' until they were all gone. They thought this was the best day ever. Then I saw a man running with a small white bag of jellies tied onto his belt. Jellies? I didn't think runners were allowed such evils as jellies, but my kids thought that it was a great idea so out came the treat box and the bowls were filled up with cola bottles and fizzy worms. They were so excited to be running down the drive, without their mother screaming 'STOP!' in panic, to hold out bowls of jellies to hundreds of heavy-breathing runners. And boy did those runners like the jellies.

All these people, moving me to tears, all this excitement at feeding them. All these causes that drove people to fight like tigers. All these tigers trying to make things better even just by a little bit and then, I SAW HER! It all happened so quickly. She passed right in front of me, she had soft silver-grey hair and the words on her T-shirt punched me in the heart. DUCHENNE. I couldn't take my eyes off her, my head turned swivel like up the road to follow her. The back of her T-shirt had her name, Margaret. I filled my lungs with air and shouted as loud as I could 'GO MARGARET!', Her left arm went up and she gave me a thumbs up. Margaret gave me a thumbs up! Margaret heard me! Most of the people I know wouldn't know what Duchenne was, but Margaret did and I did as I remembered my brother Brian who, in all his eighteen years in this world, never gave up. I felt him near. His beautiful self.

For all those running for Duchenne Muscular Dystrophy in the Dublin Marathon this year and all the other cruel and unspeakably unfair diseases and illnesses in our world that make you want to scream 'WHY?' – I will be there. I will be there with my band, beating our drums to the rhythm of your feet. We will fill our bowls with jellies, apples and oranges and so much love, to give to you. Margaret, I will look out for you and all your other friends in the rhythmic river of magic that passes by my house on the October bank holiday weekend.

9

LONG-DISTANCE DREAMS

Emma and Martin

It all started around the kitchen table of Emma and Martin's house in the summer of 2011. It was my first year to coach marathoners in a group. Thinking back to that day, I would never have imagined I would see so many runners through the training process of a marathon. With workshops, weekly meetups and online support and encouragement they turn up to their race day excited but naturally nervous. They shouldn't be really. They have prepared as well as they could possibly do and there is comfort in that. Those first runners inspired others from the group to take on the challenge. Since then every year I see new faces, and some returning ones, tempted to put their heart and soul into training for the experience of a lifetime.

Why Run a Marathon?

Why would anyone want to run a marathon just for fun? It's a valid question and one which I probably would have asked myself some years ago. For a non-runner, it's hard to appreciate the attraction of a marathon. What could possibly be so tempting when you consider the long days of training, the risk of injury, the potential blisters, the anticipation of the dreaded wall and the gourmet diet of pasta, Jelly Babies and energy gels?

Fear of missing out (FOMO) has a lot to answer for. Everyone now knows someone who has completed the marathon distance, someone who is just like them, a recreational runner who has knuckled down and put in the effort and achieved the impossible. We have all listened to friends and colleagues relay stories of long runs, emotional finish lines and the pride of the medal. These runners plant seeds of temptation in us, making us wonder if we too could take on this famous distance. If they can do it, surely I could give it a go.

The sense of pride, relief and disbelief that you feel after your first marathon makes all the training and dedication worthwhile. At the start line you doubt every bit of your training and suddenly feel the enormity of what lies ahead. You are about to run a marathon. But once you cross that finish line, you are a different person. You are a marathoner, and as anyone who has completed a marathon knows, it changes you in ways you never even imagined. It helps you believe that if you put your mind and time into anything, you can achieve the impossible.

Go Halfway First

Explaining the plan

Don't rush into the marathon distance just because your friends are doing it. If 10k has been your longest run to date, enjoy the buildup to a half marathon and learn the lessons of long distance gradually. If you can have a positive experience over a half marathon, you will be more confident, stronger and excited about taking on a marathon in the future.

I have created a twelve-week half-marathon template plan which you can adapt to suit your lifestyle and commitments. Take each week as it comes and focus on what you need to do in the week you are in. Don't panic about what might lie ahead a month down the line. Take a minute to understand how to approach each of the training sessions:

Recovery Run	A leisurely run where focus can be on technique or relaxation with the aim of starting the week well and refreshing the body from the weekend long run.
Speed Run	Your choice of one of my speed interval training sessions from page 80, or simply head out and vary your pace along the route (max. 45 minutes).
Hill Run	Find a route that is not flat and practise hill technique tips (see page 148). A consistent run of 30–40 minutes at a comfortable pace is plenty.
Long Run	This is the most important session of the week so run at a relaxed, comfortable pace. Listen to your body and take breaks if needed. Start slow and settle in.
Weekly Focus	Take time at the start of each week to read up on the relevant 'weekly focus'. A half marathon is not all about running. These extra tips will make the difference. Everything mentioned is covered in other sections of this book.

Mary's half marathon training programme

	Mon Recovery Run	Tues/Wed Speed Run	Thurs/Fri Hill Run	Weekend Long Run	Weekly Focus
Week 1	Easy 30 mins	Vary your pace	Hill training	5 miles (8k)	Make a plan
Week 2	Easy 30 mins	Vary your pace	Hill training	6 miles	Training diary
Week 3	Easy 30 mins	Vary your pace	Hill training	7 miles	Hydration
Week 4	Easy 30 mins	Vary your pace	Hill training	8 miles	Technique and hills
Week 5	Easy 30 mins	Vary your pace	Hill training	9 miles	Strength and mobility
Week 6	Easy 30 mins	Vary your pace	Hill training	10k race	Dealing with setbacks
Week 7	Easy 30 mins	Vary your pace	Hill training	10 miles	Mental training
Week 8	Easy 30 mins	Vary your pace	Hill training	Bonus week – rest	Take a break
Week 9	Easy 30 mins	Vary your pace	Hill training	10–11 miles	Know your race
Week 10	Easy 30 mins	Vary your pace	Hill training	10–12 miles	Trust the training
Week 11	Easy 30 mins	Easy 4k	Hill training	6 miles	Race day prep
Week 12	Easy 30 mins	Make lists	Easy 4k	Race day	Enjoy

Moving into Miles

Whether you are training for a half marathon or marathon, there is something strangely addictive and satisfying about the weekend long run. What runners miss about long-distance training is the routine of the long run, the shared stories and kilometres with fellow runners, the sense of satisfaction of completing the distance and the adventures and alternative routes they have travelled. Memories are truly made on these long runs, especially when it is your first time over the distance. Mini celebrations happen each week as people run the longest run of their lives, made all the more special when the sun is out and the glory is shared with others.

> NOTE: Up to now I have referenced kilometres in our training plans and race tips. As we move into longer distances I will now switch to miles for the long run sections of the plans. Although we use metric measurements generally, most of us still refer to the marathon in 'old money' – even the race organisers in Ireland will display mile markers on the marathon and half marathon routes. I have found that most of my students can manage their pace better on race day by training in miles as that's what they see on the roadside on the big day. Feel free to keep running kilometres, however, if it works better for you or if you are training for an event in central Europe. Personally, I think 26 miles sounds shorter than 42km, but the kilometres sure do go by quicker!

What a difference a day makes

The London Marathon on 17 April 2005 was the day that changed my perspective on my ability, my confidence and career. In fact, it changed my whole mindset. Signing up for a marathon was a crazy thought. At that stage I didn't know anyone who had completed a marathon. I thought marathoners were all a bunch of crazy runners.

Back at home I'm not sure many of my friends and family really understood what was involved, or what training I was doing while working in England. I do remember one particular weekend when I was home during marathon training and my dad dropped me off in the Phoenix Park. When I arranged to meet him three and a half hours later, I think it was then the penny dropped on how long a long run is.

At the time my only mentors were books, and many were inconsistent in their guidance. My bible was The Non-Runner's Marathon Trainer, *a book which I still reference many years later. I followed it weekly, compared myself to the expected, read anything and everything and tried to ignore the people who thought I was mad. I don't blame them for thinking that. I wasn't a sporty soul who would just turn up and do events like this. Most of my friends and certainly my family were not running in 2005. It was a few years before the running boom kicked off in Dublin. It was an experiment, and certainly one that was going to be a once off.*

Armed with all the knowledge and information and my sixteen-week training plan complete, I was all set for tapering; that wonderful winding down phase of training where the head starts to go crazy and the doubts kick in. I did believe I could do it, not sure how slowly, but to run the whole way was my goal – at a pace I could breathe and relax at, but without having to walk.

Two weeks to go and the buildup had started with a final long run. One minute I was looking out to sea, the next minute I was lying on the ground having tripped over the painted white line on the middle of the path. Yes, it is possible to trip over a painted line. To cut a long story short, my arm was broken. Not a major break, but a few months of rest was needed to fix it. No cast, just a bandage, as the break was at the elbow. That would rule the marathon out. I was gutted. Just when I believed I could do this race, it was being taken away from me. My friends call me Pollyanna for being an eternal optimist, and something in my head told me that I might just be able to still do it. I rested totally, and tried anything I could, from painkillers to herbal poultices to lighted candles. I cannot remember exactly how close to the race I tried a mile or two, but I did, and it wasn't too bad. I was going to attempt this.

In some ways my broken arm distracted me from the usual marathon-tapering jitters. I was so focused on the arm, any expectation I had was now reduced: I would be happy just to get through it. It was going to be a true experiment now to see how much I could do. In hindsight, sometimes the setbacks are for the best. I was more rested for marathon day and I had lifted a weight of pressure from my shoulders.

Marathon weekend arrived and one image stands out – an enormous poster over the entrance to the marathon expo that read: 'Second thoughts – it's what happens before marathons'. For me it was the moment where it all became real. This is it. I'm going to run the London Marathon.

My memories of race day are a total blur. I can remember the mass of people at the start line, the bag drop, the enormous crowds as we started and a constant stream of supporters and cheering friends and family along the way. I felt carried all the way through Greenwich and it was only when I was crossing London Bridge at thirteen miles that I realised that half was already complete. The time had flown by, it was so much easier than clock-watching in training alone. My memories of the second half are less clear, it's only as I come into the last mile that I remember the flags, the loudspeakers and Buckingham Palace.

I remember finishing comfortably and smiling and surprising myself at finishing so strongly. The strangest thing is that I have no memory of getting my medal. How can I have forgotten the one memory of the moment I had visualised for months in advance? It is funny the things we remember. My main post-race memory is walking backwards down steps into a Tube station after a post-race party with Concern, the charity I had run the race to raise funds for.

If only there were smartphones or Facebook back then, I would have a visual memory of the day. Instead I have just one photo, a lot of jumbled-up memories but a huge change in perspective.

I wonder will there ever be another day that changes my outlook on life as much? I can truly look back on that day as the one that set my life in a different direction from where it was heading. Maybe running a marathon isn't your 'life-changing' day, but the feeling of knowing you did something that you, and many others, never thought you would, is possibly the most empowering feeling there is.

Have You Got What it Takes?

While marathon is a wonderful event, character-building and life-changing for so many of us, it deserves the utmost respect and attention to detail. My goal is to help marathon runners enjoy the marathon, appreciate what is involved and cherish the whole build-up and training part as much as the race day. The marathon distance has become more accessible in recent years and it's a wonderful honour to run in the footsteps of so many great athletes and earn the title and pride of becoming a marathoner. But there is much more to a marathon than the final glory sprint to the finish line and the medal. Months of hard graft go into making sure it is a success. It takes determination, discipline and a bit of luck too. Before you get carried away with emotion and sign your life away, it's worth considering if you have what it takes to be a marathoner this year. Consider the following questions.

- **FITNESS:** If you can run 10k comfortably and have at least one to two years of running in your legs, you are in a great starting position for marathon training. Are you injury-free and confident over 10k?

- **TIME COMMITMENT:** Marathon training will involve four to five runs per week, depending on the training plan you follow. You will have one long run each week and the rest will be short runs. Do you have the time?

- **SACRIFICES:** It's important to be fresh for your long runs. Early nights and a clean diet make your training easier and your runs stronger. Can you prioritise the marathon over late nights and partying?

- **REASON:** There will be days when you don't feel like going for a run, runs where you feel like stopping, and times when you run past a park bench and wish you could sit down. You need a reason that's going to help you stay on track. Why do you want to run a marathon?

- **FINANCES:** There are many hidden costs in running a marathon. We are tempted to buy new running gear, fancy watches, sign up for other races, attend sport massage or physio, and buy everything from blister plasters to energy gels. Can you afford the investment?

- **EXPERIENCE:** Have you completed a half marathon in the past? If so, you know how your body adapts to the longer running distance and this is great preparation for what lies ahead. If you haven't, would you consider building up to a half marathon first and save the marathon for later in the year or next year? (See more about the half marathon on page 206).

- **EVENTS:** Consider what events, holidays, weddings and exams you have coming up. It's important that you can focus mentally on the marathon training and not be distracted by other events in your life. Can you organise your training around your commitments?

If I haven't turned you off yet, it's time to put pen to paper. Putting on your running shoes and clocking up the distances is not the best way to kick off your marathon training. Curb your enthusiasm for an hour and instead spend this time planning your training for the months ahead.

The Marathon Plan

All my marathon students have their full marathon training plan printed out on one page. They have a clear view of where they are going and what they need to do this week in order bring themselves closer to the marathon goal. There is no uncertainty in training as they follow the guide day by day and don't need to question if they are doing too much or too little. Their plan has mini milestones along the way which makes the marathon journey more enjoyable, motivating and, most important, structured to help avoid injury and burnout.

There is no shortage of marathon training plans available from coaches, books and running websites, so it can be overwhelming deciding on a plan. Some plans are extremely complicated while others seem very simplistic. Some plans build distance gradually while others have lots of focus on variety and speed. The right plan for you is the one that fits in with your lifestyle, fitness level and your marathon goal.

Do not commit to a plan that looks unrealistic from the start. As you progress through the weeks it will only bring stress, tension and anxiety as you cut corners in your training and your own personal life to make it work. It's true that some compromises are required to fit any marathon training plan but if you define these compromises up front there is less uncertainly. I believe a solid four day a week training plan is practical, possible and achievable for most runners. There is time for recovery between runs. It's better to be fresh and motivated for each run than feeling tired and guilty for missing extra runs.

On the following pages is a template of the type of plan I would get my runners to follow for their marathon. The distance builds gradually in the weekend runs before a wind-down phase for the final few weeks. You can see that every training run has a purpose. The weekly long run will build endurance, a hill run builds strength and confidence over different gradients, a speed run adds variety and fitness while the recovery run is a perfect opportunity to focus on technique and relaxation. Spacing these runs out across the week allows for best performance and recovery.

Be sensible and structured yet flexible in your training. It is normal for there to be unforeseen events which will impact your plan, so flexibility is key.

Explaining the plan

This is a twenty-week plan which allows a few extra weeks or 'bonus weeks' to play around with. They are nice to have as a backup if you feel your body needs a break, or if you get an unexpected invitation that means you are under pressure to do your long run.

Recovery Run	A leisurely run where focus can be on technique or relaxation with the aim of starting the week well and refreshing the body from the weekend long run.
Speed Run	Your choice of one of my speed interval training sessions from page 80, or simply head out and vary your pace along the route (max. 45 minutes). If your body is tired, revert to a leisurely 30–40 minute run.
Hill Run	Find a route that is not flat. Practise hill technique tips (see page 148) over a consistent run of 30–40 minutes at a comfortable pace. Don't push speed on this session if you have a speed run in your legs from earlier in the week.
Long Run	This is the most important session of the week so run at a relaxed, comfortable pace. Listen to your body and take breaks if needed. Start slow and settle in.
Weekly Focus	Take time at the start of each week to read up on the relevant 'weekly focus'. These extra tips will make the difference to your training, recovery and energy. Everything mentioned is covered in other sections of this book.

Aim to increase your long run distance by one mile per week. Gradual progress is the key to avoiding injury. Also include a few shorter-distance races over the months to help with race practice and motivation. Rather than overload my runners with information, I ask them to think about one element of training each week. You can see these on the weekly focus. Gradually applying new lessons and skills to their running is easier than doing everything all in one go.

Mary's marathon plan

	Mon Recovery Run Focus on Technique	Tues/Wed Speed Run Vary Your Pace	Thurs/Fri Hill Run Change It Up	Weekend Long Run Slow and Steady	Weekly Focus
Week 1	Easy 30 mins	Speed training	Hill training	7 miles	Get started
Week 2	Easy 30 mins	Speed training	Hill training	8 miles	Make a plan
Week 3	Easy 30 mins	Speed training	Hill training	9 miles	Training diary
Week 4	Easy 30 mins	Speed training	Hill training	10 miles	Work out pacing
Week 5	Easy 30 mins	Speed training	Hill training	11 miles	Hydration
Week 6	Easy 30 mins	Speed training	Hill training	12 miles	Nutrition
Week 7	Easy 30 mins	Speed training	Hill training	6 miles	Technique and hills
Week 8	Easy 30 mins	Speed training	Hill training	Half marathon race	Strength
Week 9	Easy 30 mins	Speed training	Hill training	14 miles	Flexibility
Week 10	Easy 30 mins	Speed training	Hill training	15 miles	Toilets and blisters

	Mon Recovery Run Focus on Technique	Tues/Wed Speed Run Vary Your Pace	Thurs/Fri Hill Run Change It Up	Weekend Long Run Slow and Steady	Weekly Focus
Week 11	Easy 30 mins	Speed training	Hill training	16 miles	Recovery
Week 12	Easy 30 mins	Speed training	Hill training	Bonus week – rest	Dealing with setbacks
Week 13	Easy 30 mins	Speed training	Hill training	17 miles	Mental training
Week 14	Easy 30 mins	Speed training	Hill training	18 miles	Avoid the wall
Week 15	Easy 30 mins	Speed training	Hill training	Half marathon race	Know your race
Week 16	Easy 30 mins	Speed training	Hill training	18–19 miles	Trust the training
Week 17	Easy 30 mins	40 mins marathon pace	Hill training	18–20 miles	Last long run
Week 18	Easy 30 mins	40 mins marathon pace	Hill training	12 miles	Tapering
Week 19	Easy 30 mins	40 mins marathon pace	40 mins marathon pace	6-mile marathon pace	Race day prep
Week 20	Easy 30 mins	Easy 30 mins	Easy 30 mins	Race day	Enjoy

The Long Runs

Each weekly long run should be respected and celebrated. They are huge milestones on the journey to marathon success. How we approach the weekend long run will influence how our head and our body will be prepared for the final long run of 26.2 miles. Each long run builds our confidence or dampens our spirits depending on how successful it is. Prepare well and savour the distance you're covering rather than wish it away.

The purpose of these long runs is to train your body to be on your feet for an extended length of time, so the slower the better. All your long runs should be run at a pace slightly slower than you expect to run on race day. If you don't know what pace that is, listen to your body – you should be barely out of breath when running your long run. In fact, you should be able to hold a full conversation.

When it's your first marathon everyone is curious about the long run. 'How many miles did you run this weekend?' becomes the regular Monday conversation at work. This attention can place added pressure on first-time marathoners who are now running the longest run of their life every week, but knowing the question will surely be asked might also help them through the weekend long run.

Make the long run fun rather than tedious. Get a bus somewhere and run home, arrange to meet others or just run solo and appreciate the time out. Don't be afraid to stop and walk if you need to. Not every long run will go to plan. Be conservative with your pace. Some days you will feel amazing while other long runs will leave you doubting your ability. Fear not, you will learn something from each long run. It's okay to make all your mistakes in training so that you can move towards race day knowing more about your body, your fuelling strategy and what to expect on the day. By the time you get to race weekend, all these long run experiments will leave you knowing exactly what to eat, what to wear, how to pace yourself, how to keep positive and which of your toes is most likely to get a blister.

Do the Extras

The planning and the recovery from each long run are every bit as important as the run itself. If you are doing it right, the long run might feel like it takes over more of your weekend than just a Saturday morning. Being relaxed, rested, prepared and confident starting your run, knowing your pace, your route and when you are going to eat and drink on the way are all key to finishing your long run strong and positive. Rest does not mean dancing in high heels, spending hours walking around town or working on your feet for the day. Your muscles repair while you sleep and as all athletes know well, sleep and rest is considered training too.

There is more behind the scenes than just running, however. Allow time in your training plan for strength and conditioning, flexibility work and recovery. Build a few minutes of strength and flexibility into your daily routine. Many of these exercises are easy to do while watching TV, playing with the kids or even while waiting for a bus. Work on hip stability and core strength and aim to keep the entire body as flexible as possible as the mileage increases. Pay particular attention to the areas of your body you have noticed feeling tight or stiff on your long runs (see Chapter 7). So much of what can go wrong in a marathon is down to lack of preparation. There is an element of luck with everything, but you can do a lot by minding your body each week.

Marathoner Q & A

Q. What time should I aim for?

A. We often pick a desired marathon finishing time based on what we consider to be a 'good' marathon time or the time we know someone else has completed. The truth is, unless you have done a marathon before it is very hard to predict an exact finishing time. As a first timer I wouldn't commit to any time goal but instead set a goal to enjoy the training as well as the race day. Once you know your marathon body better, you can aim to beat that time next year if you like.

I have met many a marathoner disappointed with their first marathon just because they finished a few minutes slower than they expected. They forget they have run a marathon and instead focus on what they have not achieved. Your approach to finishing times can really impact your stress on marathon day. Indeed, you will often get asked 'what time are you aiming for?' during training but just smile and say, 'I'm just hoping to get around in one piece' and avoid any further discussion on the subject. The more people who know the time in your head, the more pressure it is.

As you get closer to race day you will be able to predict generally what pace you will be able to sustain, and you can plan a bit better then, but whatever you do, don't become obsessed with the numbers if you are taking on the distance for the first time.

Q. Where is the nearest loo?

A. It's the thought on many marathoners' minds as they head out for their long run. Knowing you can go if you need to will make you more relaxed and often that in itself will make you less nervous. If you need to go to the toilet on a run, then go. It is not cheating on a long run to stop and go to the toilet. Bring along toilet paper if you need to. In your training run, know where the toilets are, the trees that are big enough to hide behind (yes, we all do this) and the petrol stations and places you will pass if you do need to go in. Also consider what might be triggering the urge. On race day, there will be plenty of toilets at the start line and scattered along the route (see also page 166).

Q. Will I lose toenails?

A. The feet certainly can feel the weight of marathon training but I'm still holding on to all my toenails. Blisters are more common as the mileage increases. They are triggered most frequently by friction and heat. Wet weather and soggy socks don't help either. Some people use blister plasters on areas where they know they are prone to blister. Others use medical tape or Vaseline to protect the most sensitive areas. Personally I have found that an area that is prone to blisters tends to toughen up as the weeks go on and hard skin develops around it. Some people say to keep the skin soft, but I've found that letting these hard areas develop makes the blister less of an issue. It's also worth noting how you are tying your shoe laces. Make sure your foot is not shifting and moving inside the shoe. This should also help you avoid those lovely black toenails which may be painful or not. (Some runners keep their toenails permanently painted in bright nail varnish to hide these features!)

Q. What is chafing?

A. Some day you will let out a scream in the shower as you feel the burn of the water hitting an area that has chafed. It might be caused by sports bra, shorts or even the underarm of your T-shirt – you will learn very quickly what areas are most sensitive and what clothing causes the problem. Moisture and friction are also a problem here. There are anti-chafing creams on the market or you can use basic Vaseline to protect the area. I have found that medical tape can work well too. It all depends on the body part. Old sports bras seem to be a big issue (it took me a while to work that out and in the interim I was wearing tape over the areas that rubbed). I recommend having your 'long run outfit' planned right down to your socks and underwear so you know there are no potential friction areas. Wear this outfit on your long run only and save those clothes just for the weekly long run so they stay in good shape for the duration of your training. I thankfully can say I've never experienced the 'bleeding nipple', which is another form of friction and chafing, but rumour has it that plasters work well for the boys by providing an extra layer in the area.

Q. How do I carry everything?

A. It is awkward and uncomfortable holding a water bottle throughout a long run. Not only that, it tightens your fist, which will impact your shoulder. Ideally we should avoid carrying anything in our hands when running. There are lots of options now for runners to carry their stash of provisions when on the run. Small bottles on a belt, a circular bottle which you hold via a hole in the centre that goes on your wrist, backpacks with water straws and much more. See what works for you. Consider how much you realistically need to carry. If you are running laps, leave the bottle on your car, on a tree branch etc, and pick it up each time you pass it. It's a lot easier to carry a few euro and nip into a shop for water. For the added extras of keys, food and maybe even toilet paper, there are neat little waist bags which can carry a lot for a small size and most runners will use these for long distance. You could even pin a little bag of sweets to your shorts, just watch you don't prick yourself when removing them – we are not as mentally sharp as we might think towards the end of the long run.

Stay in the Moment

Even though the marathon is the only thing on your mind, it is important not to look too far forward to race day. Try to just focus on the week you are in. Every long run is a stepping stone to get you to next week, and ultimately to the marathon distance, in good shape. Try not to get overwhelmed. Long-distance running entails tricking your body into always focusing on the positive and staying present with your run. Letting doubts creep in can impact your posture, confidence, motivation and commitment to the training. There is no point wasting your energy worrying about the long miles that lie ahead later in the plan.

Avoid thinking about everything that might go wrong on race day. It's a privilege to be in a position to line up at a marathon start line, yet so many never truly enjoy the marathon buildup as they are so focused on factors which are outside their control. There is no point worrying about the weather, the pace of a friend or the potential of having an upset stomach on the day. If you must, make a list of all your worries. By the time race day arrives you will be a completely different runner from the one you are now, and those worries may no longer be a concern. To stop the anxiety, take an hour out, write down everything that might go wrong and what you are going to do if that happens on race day. You will make a more rational decision now than you will at twenty miles.

Distract yourself from your doubts by becoming excited about what might go right and all the new challenges that lie ahead. Every day ask yourself if what you are doing is helping or hindering your marathon success. A series of simple choices and decisions will all add up to a strong, confident and successful runner come marathon day.

Another Marathon?

If you already have a marathon medal, I wonder why you are contemplating another one? Maybe you have unfinished business or maybe you just loved it so much before that you want to recreate the feeling. One thing is certain, you know what lies ahead between now and the finish line. Although you won't be running the longest run of your life every weekend, you do have the benefit of experience. You know what works for your stomach, your ideal marathon starting pace and which shorts don't chafe. All these valuable lessons learnt give you a head start on the first-timers. But having the medal already can also make you complacent about training. It is often harder to train for a marathon that's not your first. Motivation can be an issue as the excitement, fear and anticipation may not be as high as first time around. You may possibly now have a time target and put more pressure on yourself than last time around.

After each marathon, I write down my 'lessons learnt', and try to remember those in the next event. It doesn't always happen but in general, we learn from our mistakes, and as long as each mistake is a new one, then I'm happy. Marathon running does not have to be about running PBs all the time, and finishing thinking you never want to run again. The feel-good factor of running a marathon at a pace where you feel strong, comfortable and can take in your surroundings is immense. In some of my past marathons I've made enjoyment my goal rather than trying to aim for a personal best. Work out what your goal is for this marathon and have a few backup plans too.

Avoid the Wall

A well-fuelled runner reduces their risk of hitting the dreaded marathon 'wall'. If the body does not get the fuel it needs, it slows down unnecessary processes, such as running, in order to keep our essential systems functioning properly. We can feel weak, dizzy and ultimately our pace, focus and performance decreases. If you have watched the latter stages of a marathon you most certainly have seen some runners who could have planned their fuelling strategy better.

In its simplest terms, we lose water, salt and sugar when we run long distance. The sugar powers our muscles and through sweat we lose salt and water as the body works to keep itself cool. How we choose to replenish our body with these three components is a personal decision, but it is important to recognise why we need to take it all seriously.

Regardless of what you eat the night before or the morning of the marathon you will need to top up your water, salt and sugar during the run. I believe that eating and drinking little and often while running has helped me avoid hitting the wall over my years of marathons, but it takes time, experience and dedication to work out your own optimal nutrition strategy. A first-time marathon runner has an opportunity each week this summer to work out exactly what food agrees with their body and help build their confidence, strength and endurance for the autumn marathon. Some runners can eat and run concurrently while others find that liquids only are what works for them. Many stomachs are sensitive, especially when they are jigging up and down for hours on a long run. Don't rely on what works for a friend. Nothing beats experimenting with different foods yourself.

The Marathon Menu

The only thing a long-distance runner thinks about more than running is food. When we are not planning our next run, our mind is on our next meal. For any first-timer who has notions of losing weight while marathon training, you might find it more difficult than you think. Most marathon runners are pretty hungry creatures. Making the right decisions about food can make a huge difference to our running performance, focus and recovery.

For eating on the run some people like to stick with natural food and find that fruit, nuts and homemade bars or snacks help them through. While most would agree that natural food is best, we need to think practically and fuel our bodies with something that is convenient to carry as well as gentle on the stomach.

There has been a boom in portable running snacks in recent years, and you can now find a wide array of endurance food products on the market aimed at helping a runner with energy, repair and concentration. From sweets with added salt and caffeine, to bars, gels, energy drinks and dissolvable tablets, there is endless choice of products available. It can be overwhelming to know what to choose. The truth is that not every product will work for you. For example, some people thrive on caffeine sweets while many with a sensitive stomach need to avoid caffeine or they will spend a long time in the portaloos en route (see also page 167).

Complete marathon nutrition involves more than just what you eat on the run. Breakfast, post-run snacks and what we eat during the week all contribute to our energy and our recovery from long runs. There is no need to overcomplicate midweek food and hydration. Simply remember that what you feed your body with will be used to fuel your run and repair your body afterwards. We can avoid race weekend anxiety around food if we answer all our gourmet questions during training (see Chapter 7).

The Final Countdown

The tapering phase of marathon training aims to get the body and mind fresh for marathon day. Over these final few weeks of training, the body repairs itself from months of long runs and builds energy resources to fuel marathon day. This phase of training sounds like it should be easy as it mainly focuses on rest, recovery, eating well and building confidence and strength. However, many runners are not good at sitting still and accepting that less is more at this stage.

We have indeed more time on our hands, but rather than relaxing this is often spent thinking up worst-case scenarios for marathon day. It starts with the phantom pains, the heavy legs, the feeling of losing fitness, general lethargy and of course the added competitive marathon banter between friends and club mates. It's no wonder that by race day there are so many runners doubting their ability. Those negative voices shout louder as we get closer to marathon day.

We need to silence the negative thoughts and convince ourselves that we are ready for the big day.

It may sound surprising but first-time marathoners have a huge advantage over everyone else. You are not carrying around a time on the clock from a previous marathon. This is going to be your fastest marathon to date and possibly your only marathon. In order to make the most of it, here are a few things that will make it extra special and keep you calm and relaxed in the days and hours before the big day.

Marathon Checklist

1 Review your training log

Look back over all you have achieved in the last few months. Remember all the obstacles you have overcome. Think of all the runs you didn't think you would do – but you did. You have trained well for the marathon; stop doubting yourself. Trust the training.

2 Plan your food for the week

Think about everything you will need for the weekend race. Write out a list of the breakfast food, the race food, the pre-race dinner food, everything you need to get into your kitchen before the weekend. Remember hydration early in the week too. Don't leave it till the race morning.

3 Create a checklist of everything you need on race day

Avoid the anxiety of thinking you have forgotten something by taking twenty minutes to write down everything you need to bring with you on marathon day. Make a list, review it each day, and ensure you have everything you need.

4 Visualise your race

Train like an elite athlete to get your head in the race zone. Picture your race morning, your starting pace, your route along the marathon course and your finish-line smile. Repeat this daily until you actually believe you can do it (see page 188).

5 Organise your supporters

Nothing beats the buzz of a meeting a friend or family member along the route jumping up and down cheering you on; nothing is worse than missing them when you get distracted for a few seconds. Arrange in advance where to meet them and what they will have with them (see page 196).

6 Sleep and rest

Get good sleep early in the week. Even if you are nervous at the weekend and struggle to sleep then, you will have banked good-quality sleep from early in the week and you will be fine on race day.

7 Get your name printed on your T-shirt

Yes, I know it sounds a bit cheesy but trust me, it is one of the single best things you can do. As people cheer your name along the route, it will motivate and encourage you all the way along.

8 Work out your race strategy

Do you know what pace you are going to start at? At what mile will you take your first gel/drink? Are you going to take walk breaks? What is your pacing strategy? Plan out your race pace and fuelling mile by mile. Mile fourteen is not the time to decide you have run the first thirteen miles too fast.

And on race day itself...

TAKE IT ALL IN – nothing beats the 'first marathon' feeling. This will be your fastest marathon; it may also be your only marathon. Aim to enjoy it. That should be the first priority.

BE GRATEFUL – you are so lucky to be able to do this so enjoy it! There are so many people who would love to be in a position to run a marathon. You are one of the lucky ones. Appreciate the fact you can line up at the start line. That, in itself, is a privilege. Thank the volunteers and appreciate the supporters who help to make the day so special.

START SLOWLY – there are no medals for running the first 10k. It's so easy to get carried away by the atmosphere at the start line. Your first mile will feel very easy, and it's tempting to run faster. Don't. It will catch up with you later. Decide in advance the pace you will run your first mile – and stick to it!

BREAK IT INTO SMALL CHUNKS – avoid getting overwhelmed with the numbers. Take it one mile at a time. Only think about the mile that you are in. You will have plenty of time to worry about twenty miles when you get there.

TRUST YOUR TRAINING – don't compare yourself to anyone else. No two runners have had the same path to the marathon, so you cannot compare training, times or result. We all overcome different obstacles on our marathon journey. There will always be faster runners (who do less training than you). The only competition is with yourself.

DON'T STRESS ABOUT THE TIME IT TAKES – do you really want to finish your first marathon and feel disappointed with yourself? Make sure any time goal you set is realistic, and not based on someone else's time. There is always the next marathon to beat your time. You really don't know how your body is going to feel at 22 miles – so be sensible and realistic.

SMILE – if you are feeling tired, stiff, in pain, nervous, anxious or generally overwhelmed along the route just slow down, relax and smile. It's amazing what a smile can do to trick the body into feeling better. Not only that, more people cheer you when you smile, your body will relax, and you might just start to feel better!

MANAGE THE DOUBTS – there will undoubtedly come a point in the marathon where you want to stop, you wonder why you are doing this and you feel your confidence suddenly decrease. Accept this is going to happen at some point, and possibly a few times, but I promise it's a temporary dip. Plan in advance what you are going to say to yourself when this happens. And practise saying it to yourself. The wave of negativity will pass, but you can help this by reminding yourself of the hard work you have put in and picturing yourself feeling strong and finishing the race.

How to Pace Your Marathon

The best way to sabotage your marathon is to start too fast. It's so easy to get carried away with the pace at the start, you feel fresh, you haven't run in ages and adrenaline is pumping. Indeed, if you are feeling good at twenty miles pick up your pace, but never change your pacing plans (to go faster) in the first few hours of the marathon.

Use your long runs as a guide if it is your first marathon. You can go at the pace you have managed the long runs at, or a slight bit quicker. I would suggest being conservative, however, at the start. Be disciplined in the first half and you will enjoy it all the more.

Practise your marathon pace in the last few weeks of marathon training. Running three to four miles on a weeknight at marathon pace should feel very comfortable and it is great practice to resist the urge to push on. Doing these training sessions, you will come to recognise the marathon pace and find it easier to hold yourself back on marathon day for the first half when you feel rested, fresh and enthusiastic.

Sometimes, there is a chance you have a bad day and your predetermined marathon pace feels breathless and uncomfortable. In this situation it is wise to pull back the pace and get comfortable again. It takes discipline to do this and it can be demoralising. By reducing pace early in the run, you give your body a chance to recover. You may get a second wind, but pushing through at a faster pace, just because on paper you are supposed to do it, may well burn more energy than necessary too soon and is a fast track to hitting the wall.

Official race pacers on the day can also take the effort out of having to think about pace (once you choose to run with the correct one). They are very supportive and will help you stay at your pace. However, it can be very congested on the road close to the pacers. Personally, I would run about two hundred metres behind them and keep them within that distance so I have the space of the road as well as the draw of the pacing balloons. If, like me, you lose the ability to do maths when running, you

might like pacing bands which you can wear on your wrist. The band gives you the time you should be passing through each mile marker based on your target timing. Alternatively, write a few numbers on your arm to help you – your three-mile time, your six-mile time, your half-way time.

Your marathon pace will feel incredibly slow on race day. It should for the first few miles anyhow. Burning your fuel too early by running too fast will increase your chances of hitting the wall later. Avoid the wall, run comfortably and feel strong in the closing stages. That is the ideal way to finish your marathon. There is nothing as powerful as overtaking people in the final miles of the marathon.

As I have mentioned many times, your first marathon is not the one to have a time goal. There is always next year to put on a time pressure. For those of you who are running your second, third, fourth, etc. marathon, it's helpful to have a few backup goals. If you know your 'A' goal, but this ideal realistic marathon time becomes out of reach, it's easy to become deflated. Instead, have a 'B' goal and a 'C' goal to work towards. The 'B' goal may be five to ten minutes slower than your 'A' goal; your 'C' goal might be your time from last year or a time that you know is very manageable (if everything goes well on the day). There is always the risk you do not meet any of these goals, but having a few options is a lot better than working to one number only and then losing all motivation to finish once this becomes out of reach.

As the years go on you may want to challenge yourself more by using some more advanced pacing strategies, but you need to look after your pace for your first few marathons, or you won't still be running marathons and enjoying them into the future. Build your base, and you will learn something new about your pace and endurance each time. You may finish the marathon thinking that you have more in you and you could have run a little faster. The day after the marathon (or any race for that matter), we all think we could have pushed on more. That's only normal.

'My aim was to complete a marathon before my fiftieth birthday last year. What blew me away was how much I enjoyed it and how happy I was doing it plus the friends in the Forget The Gym group I made along the way. You had me so well prepared mentally, physically and nutritionally that my second half was faster than my first. It has given me a confidence within myself that no matter what hits me, if I can do a marathon I can do anything, and I think it definitely helped me recover and want to return after my bike accident last year. Thank you again so much, feel free to share the photo with any would-be marathoners about to start their amazing adventure.'
Jill

Looking Good
Running Chicks
Forget The Gym.ie
Trust the
Training
You Can Do It
Forget The

After the Marathon

For one week of your life you feel like a celebrity with the compliments, the goodwill and the amazement of all your friends and family that you actually competed the marathon. Well done you – you are a marathoner and I hope you have had the chance to let it all sink in. As the adrenaline starts to wear off, and maybe the aches and pains kick in, there are few things you can do ...

WRITE IT ALL DOWN – you will forget so quickly how it all felt, so get a notebook and write down your experience of the marathon. It will be fantastic to look over in the future when the memories feel more like a dream.

KEEP MOBILE – keep the body loose by taking some easy walks, finishing by stretching. Don't overdo it; the marathon takes a lot out of the body and you will be prone to injury and illness this week if you do too much.

RUN FOR FUN – it's pretty normal to say 'never again' after the marathon, but in a few days, you may be looking up new races. Please do not book in for another marathon for at least six months, but ideally one year. Give your body time to recover and enjoy the post-marathon buzz for now. For the next month run simply for fun, not worrying about following a training schedule. That said, you might not feel like running at all.

AVOID THE POST-MARATHON BLUES – it's very common for the trauma, stress and the pressure of the marathon to turn you off running for a while. Everything has been focused on one day, and now it has passed we can feel at a loss. Days after the event, runners often feel a void in their lives. Try to focus on something other than running. Do some of the things you missed out on due to your training.

DON'T DWELL ON THE NEGATIVES – very few people have the perfect marathon day. Be grateful that you could take part and line up on race day. We all learn something from every race so look for the positives in your training and your race day.

BE GOOD TO YOURSELF – enjoy nice hot baths, good food, plenty of sleep and good times with friends and family – don't forget to hang your medal on your Christmas tree too! Every year it will give you a smile when you take it out of the box of decorations. Of course, you might prefer to have it hanging on the wall all year round. Whatever happens to the medal, it is yours and you deserve it.

10

CREATE YOUR FUTURE

The Pressure to be Better

You will never be as young as you were yesterday so trying to be the runner you were years ago will only lead to disappointment and possibly injury. It can take away your love for running if all you do is keep your eye on the past. Being realistic about our future running potential is important.

While some runners are yet to reach their peak in terms of speed and strength, others look back on their glory days with great memories. The frustration of not being as fast as you used to be can take the novelty of running away from many passionate and dedicated runners. Runners who were successful in their teenage and early adult years may never get close to their personal best again and motivation and enthusiasm can dip. If you are struggling with this, imagine how hard it must be for an aging elite athlete whose identity is constantly being measured by running numbers.

If running is always a pressure or stress we can grow to resent it and it may become something we 'have to do' rather than something we 'choose to do'. We can feel we are failing if speed becomes our only measure of success and that in turn can prevent us from keeping on running as we don't see ourselves as a 'good' runner anymore.

Consider diets and how they take the love of food away from many people. Just as we can view food as only calories rather than appreciating all the other pleasures it can bring, sometimes we are guilty of only focusing on running as performance and speed when there are actually many more benefits to the body than just being our fastest self. That is only one component of the magic of running.

Keep the Love for Running

We need targets that are realistic yet challenging. Seeing improvements is what makes us reach further and keep lacing up our running shoes. We need to keep the joy in running and find a measure that is reasonable to chase. There are age group categories in most races and in parkrun there is an age-grading system that allows you to compare your time against others, allowing for age and gender. There are not many sports that are lifelong. However, make sure you don't outgrow your love of running by becoming disillusioned with unrealistic expectations.

If a lifetime personal best is not appropriate for you to aim for right now, maybe you could create a more realistic and personal target. My current favourite is the PB created by our coach Aoife at Forget The Gym after she returned to running after having her first baby. Her PBPB (post-baby-personal best) became her new number. Her lifetime PB seemed like a mountain to climb. Instead she focused on making gradual progress on her PBPB which was more rewarding, achievable and enjoyable. Consider what life events you have experienced that may have impacted your running. If your lifetime PB is a distant memory, should you set a different target? You can choose to create any timeline for your new PB. You could have a 'post-50 PB', a 'post-Illness PB' or maybe a 'post-retirement PB'! Leave the past where it is and create a PB that you can bring into the future with you.

As we grow older I don't think we should expect to have to retire the running shoes. Instead I suggest we look at new ways to make running work for us. When do you see yourself stopping running and why? Maybe you feel you want to run a marathon and then give it up. That's fine, no one is saying you need to run for ever. But wouldn't it be great to have the option of being able to?

The Lifelong Runner

I imagine an older woman enjoying running by the sea, smiling, relaxed and light on her feet. The sun is shining, the beach is empty and the lady floats along taking in the view and appreciating her ability to run and everything that is around her. She is looking comfortable yet strong. She is pain-free yet aware of her aging body and will finish her run with some mobility exercises and a healthy breakfast with friends at a local café. This is how I picture my running future, yet I know that if I don't look after my running body I won't be able to live this dream.

I also envisage myself as one of those older ladies in a flowery swimming hat who does a daily sea dip all year round despite the weather. That I am much further away from achieving. I would currently be reluctant to take a sea dip in the Irish summer but we can all dream. Maybe someday I'll meet the right people who will help me become this lady. My subconscious at least is looking for a way to dip my toes into this cold water.

I think both of these ladies are women who are active, mobile and vibrant. The body may be aging but is staying strong and fresh and not giving up. I understand that there is a lot to be said about living in the moment, but I believe if we look ahead to where we want to go we have the ability to set ourselves on the right path at the very least. I want running, and coaching, to be a part of my life long term so if this is going to happen I need to protect my body, adapt my running and set myself up for success. The number of marathons or specific times in races doesn't drive me too much at the moment. I'd love running to bring me places, to go on travels and introduce me to new people.

However you define your running success, in order to get there you need to think about more than just kilometres. Motivation, enjoyment, strength, recovery, good technique and a positive mindset will keep you running well into the future. Running isn't just about fitness. It's motivation, camaraderie, shared goals and memories as well as the building of bonds between the generations that we could all do with a little more of in our lives. Consider everything you have learnt from running so far. Think about the people it has brought into your life, the places you have been and the challenges you have overcome.

As I write this final paragraph I'm sitting here at my kitchen table in my running gear, legs restless to close the laptop and get some fresh air. Aren't we so lucky to have such freedom on our doorstep? The only downside is that I'm sure I'll think of about ten extra things I should have written about once I'm out on the winding running path that gives me all my best ideas. If that's the only downside of running, I'll take it.